Visionary Trader

How to be a Winner in the Stock Market

Ron Chicone

Visionary Trader
Copyright © 2019 by Ron Chicone
ISBN: 978-1-7320865-4-8
Library of Congress Control Number: 2019908606

This is not a fictional book. Everything in this book is factual and done to the author's best ability.

All rights reserved. No part of this book may be reproduced, stored in a retrieval system, or transmitted in any form or by any means without the prior written permission of the author, except by a reviewer who may quote brief passages in a review printed in a newspaper, magazine, or journal.

Cover Art: Shutterstock

Printed in the United States of America

La Maison Publishing, Inc.
Vero Beach, Florida
The Hibiscus City
lamaisonpublishing@gmail.com

Author Credentials

- Over thirty years as a registered Advisor with Advantage Capital Corp.
- Four years United States Air force.
- Reenlisted United States Army.
- Entrepreneur various enterprises.
- Dance studios
- Chain of Beauty Salons
- Night Clubs
- Manufacturing plant etc.

Disclaimer and Waiver of Claims

We Are Not Financial Advisors or a Broker/Dealer: Neither Ron Chicone nor any of his officers, employees, representatives, agents, or independent contractors are, in such capacities, licensed financial advisors, registered investment advisers, or registered broker-dealers. Ron Chicone does not provide investment or financial advice or make investment recommendations, nor is it in the business of transacting trades, nor does it direct client commodity accounts or give commodity-trading advice tailored to any particular client's situation. Nothing contained in this communication constitutes a solicitation, recommendation, promotion, endorsement, or offer by Ron Chicone of any particular security, transaction, or investment. Securities Used as Examples: The securities used in this example is used for illustrative purposes only. Ron Chicone does not recommend that you buy or sell these securities Past performance shown in examples may not be indicative of future performance. Return on Investment "ROI" Examples: The securities used in this example is for illustrative purposes only. The calculation used to determine the return on investment "ROI" does not include the number of trades, commissions, or any other factors used to determine ROI. The ROI calculation measures the profitability of investment and, as such, there are alternate methods to calculate/express it. All information provided is for educational purposes only and does not imply, express, or guarantee future returns. Past performance shown in examples may not be indicative of future performance. Investing Risk: Trading securities can involve high risk and the loss of any funds invested. Investment information provided may not be appropriate for all investors and is provided without respect to individual investor financial sophistication, financial situation, investing time horizon, or risk tolerance. Options Trading Risk: Options trading is generally more complex than stock trading and may not be suitable for some investors. Granting options and some other options strategies can result in the loss of more than the original amount invested. Before trading options, a person should review the document Characteristics and Risks of Standardized Options, available from your broker or any exchange on which options are traded. No part of this presentation may be copied, recorded, or rebroadcast in any form without the prior written consent of Ron Chicone.

Ron Chicone

EXORDIUM

Critics do not have a place in this compendium.

It is not the critic who counts, or the man who points out a small hollow error that means next to nothing and gives his sagging soul a reentry into the essence of life and lifts his ego for the moment. Yet he has no earth shattering enlightenment for the human race.

It is a small man that points out how the strong man stumbles, or where the doer of deeds could have done them better.

The credit belongs to the man who is actually in the arena, who strives valiantly, who errs, and who comes short again and again.

Remember, there is no effort without error and shortcoming. Hail the person who actually strives to do the deeds; who knows great enthusiasms, and great devotions; who spends himself in a worthy cause; who at the best knows in the end the triumph of high achievement, and who at the worst, if he fails, at least fails while daring greatly, so that his place shall never be with those cold and timid souls who neither know victory nor defeat.—Theodore Roosevelt

Today is all of your Tomorrows

When the shadow of decay is all around, turn to the East, where brightening inevitably occurs.

Yesterday today was the future and tomorrow is the promise.

The missteps of the past once atoned for can never be repeated, if you accept that within you lie the seeds of success and happiness.

Today is the moment in time cultivation takes place and tomorrow we reap the whirlwind of opportunity.

Remember, today comes every day and if you missed yesterday than try it again,

Today comes again tomorrow — Ron Chicone

Prologue

My experience has taught me that buyers are optimists and sellers are liars and those that hold for the long term are dreamers and they always come late or never show for the party.

The predilection of the vast majority of the world population is status quo. Weary and of no-consequence people. For them the world offers very little challenge, nor do they want an encounter of any type. But the world is full of contests, conflicts, and struggles. Participation in the Arena of life is a must if you are to advance to the end result. If you haven't grabbed the Golden ring encrusted with diamonds, it will eventually be too late. That old man or old women is patiently waiting for you. The train is leaving the station. The party is over and those that are still at the station and picking over the residue of the revelry, are left with what might-have-been. How sad!

The person that is the life of the party will never be late, is eager to learn, knows that he doesn't know, wants more of everything life has to offer, has imagination, can fantasize and except for an occasional conversant informed witticism that contributes to the occasion, keeps his/her damn mouth shut. When you are talking you are not listening and more than likely wasting your time and the time of the imparter of a vast amount of knowledge that could potentially increase your skills and your ability to advance your self-interests.

The object of this book is to give knowledge not readily obtained elsewhere. This book is dedicated to those that want. Yes I said, "Want." I mean, to "want" everything that you desire in life and make it available to you the easy way.

Many of you are thinking, isn't this book about money. Well, yes it is, but it's also about psychology and personality and expansiveness and at the same time personal limits. It's about successes, mistakes, embarrassments, and the many times you have said "why did I say that, what the hell was I thinking".

It's hard to think of something money cannot buy except an entrance to your maker. But I am not a theologian. The doctrine you subscribe to must be between you and your creator.

I believe this missive will be your key to a rich and satisfying life.

Remember the train is leaving the station. You have the ability to catch it. Don't be late.

The pot-of-Gold is now, not at the end of the Rainbow.

The Truth

What this book is not:

1) A training ground for neophyte investors.
2) A love story; Enhancing that statement means never fall in love with a stock because it will never love you back.
3) A systems magnet.
4) A magic carpet.
5) It will not make you dependent on this or any method of investing.
6) Other than the cost of the book, it will not badger you to spend one penny on some method that portends to have all the answers.

What this book is:

1) An allegorical treasure that opens and expands your mental capacity.
2) A map that communicates and conveys pathways to unencumbered truths concerning investing, without the dogma and falsehoods categorized as an irrefutable investing positive.
3) Simple in its complexity.
4) An advocate of investing pugilism as practiced in the real arena.
5) An amplification of action as applied to accomplishment.
6) A compendium of psychological points of call that have the effect of driving you forward to success.

Table of Contents

$ CHAPTER ONE $ 1
THE GREAT STOCK TRADERS OF THE PAST 1
- Jim Fisk Jr. 3
- Robber Barons 5
- Jekyll Island Club and the Federal Reserve 10
- The Grand Dinning Hall at Jekyll Island Club 10
- Jessie Livermore 35
- J. P. Morgan 44
- Ziegfeld Follies—Jesse's wife—Dorothy 50
- Trading Secrets of Jesse Lauriston Livermore 58
- William Crapo Durant 66
- Bernard Baruch 77
- Richard Whitney 85
- James Buchanan Brady 97

$ CHAPTER TWO $ 118
- Psycho-Cybernetics and The Silva Mind Control Method 118
- THE SECRET 124
- THE IMPORTANCE OF IMAGINATION 125
- USING RATIONAL THINKING AND RELAXATION 127

$ CHAPTER THREE $ 135

The Search for Investments 135

Finding Potential Investments 135

Valuation 141

$ CHAPTER FOUR $ 146

Finding Growth Stocks 146

Trading methods of Jesse Livermore 159

$ CHAPTER FIVE $ 163

Short Sales 163

Manages Inflation 171

Supervises the Banking System 173

Maintains the Stability of the Financial System 175

Provides Banking Services 175

    Who Owns the Fed 177

    Role of the Fed Chair 178

    How the Fed Affects You 179

Bear Markets 190

$ CHAPTER SIX $ 195

Options 195

$ CHAPTER SEVEN $ 211

Victory 211

$ CHAPTER EIGHT $ 223

Life is Lived only Once 223

$ CHAPTER NINE $ 226
Finding Growth Stocks 226
$ CHAPTER TEN $ 233
Ramifications of Old Age 233
Addendum 236

Visionary Trader

$ CHAPTER ONE $

THE GREAT STOCK TRADERS OF THE PAST

The past is prologue, or what has gone before; and it is anticipation of what is to come. The future is coda, meaning the ending. When we talk about the past, it's all the things that have happened to make you the person you have become. When we talk about the future, it is the many things that happen in your lifetime with the ending being death.

Looking at it in that way makes you aware that all of life may be just preparation for your demise. Whether true or not, more than likely you have been practicing for the thing you really want to do; whether you realize it or have not been sufficiently aware of your abilities.

Society has always had a great admiration for the dreamers among us. Dreams have been called the incubation period of success. Looking back at your early years, when your instructor was presenting and pontificating about some abstract subject that held little interest for you, I'm sure your thoughts were elsewhere, focused on something that held more of a fascination.

Did you find that your daydreams were of greater interest to you than what your teacher was currently preaching? That was not something you should have been doing.

If I may! That is exactly what you should have been doing.

There will be a multitude of relatives and family, friends and everyday folks who explain to you why your grades should be better and how important to your future education will be. Let not your heart be troubled by this well intended vector.

Much of the paths followed by those that have found nirvana throughout their life were dictated by wants and dreams. They seemed to float above all the turbulence that their activism created. This formula was followed by every successful entrepreneur that I have studied in whatever field of endeavor finally was chosen. Not only did they throw convention aside, but trouble and turmoil seemed to follow them.

I have promised you an easy way to riches, and because I have been a participant in the arena of life and never just a spectator, I have experienced much of the troubles and conflict in what has been a life of consequence. I know that I can show you how to avoid future potholes in the road and give you the ability to grab the Golden ring the easy way.

Always follow your dreams. They are there for a reason, and that will be the foundation of all the success you have in the future.

Now I have revealed the first secret to victory in the pursuit of money.

Pay attention because each person that I present gives their passport to the Garden of Eden. Be aware of the cornerstones at the end of each cameo. These are the stepping-stones to success.

Jim Fisk Jr.

Aka. Jubilee Jim
Born April 1, 1835

Though uneducated, his commitment was to generating massive amounts of money and influence. Through various schemes and alliance's he was able to acquire, along with partner Jay Gould, controlling interest in the Erie Railroad.

He had an open alliance with Boss Tweed who controlled Tammany Hall in New York, who in turn controlled Politicians, and unabashedly used bribery on other gentleman of influence, thereby manipulating the outcome of business interests that involved Jim Fisk.

Jubilee Jim was both loved and feared depending on whom you asked or whose calf was being gored.

Jim was no stranger to controversy; in 1864 he was hired as a stockbroker by Daniel Drew. They teamed up to depose Cornelius Vanderbilt, who was the boss of Erie Railroad. Later, Jim turned on Drew and collaborated with the prominent Jay Gould to become general operating partners of Erie.

Jay Gould

Cornelius Vanderbilt

Robber Barons

Not all of Jim's schemes resulted in profit. He received his come-uppance in a big way when he and Gould tried to corner the Gold market. Believing they could make a deal with President Grant, who had a notoriously corrupt administration.

President Grant

Gould and Fisk approached President Grant to halt weekly gold sales that he was using to pay off the massive debt the Civil War had created, while both of them bought massive amounts of the glittering metal. Grant eventually reneged on the deal causing gold and the country to regress into a mini-recession and Fisk and Gould to lose a substantial amount of their investments.

Unscrupulous should have been Jim's middle name. He made enormous amounts of money trading with both the North and the South during the Civil War.

Josie Mansfield
Considered voluptuous by Golden Age standards

Edward Stokes

Jubilee Fiske was a player, to use today's idiom, as far as the fairer sex was concerned. He married a woman named Lucy Moore, but he never lived with her, and she tolerated his many affairs mainly because she was in love with another woman.

The woman that Fisk was romancing for a period of time by the name of Josie Mansfield went on to be the cause of many predicaments and difficulties in his life.

This relationship scandalized New York and it became more scandalized when she of presumably high standards fell in love with a former colleague of Jim's. His name was Edward Stokes and fool that Stokes was, fell head over heels in love and in fact left his wife and children for her. Mansfield then dropped Fisk who did not seem to feel any remorse.

These two icons of virtue decided to blackmail Jubilee Jim, threatening the publication of letters written by Jim to Josie.

There was a little more to this story:

In 1865, Stokes was operating an oil refinery in Brooklyn at Hunter's Point. He sought funding and acquired two investors, Henry Harley and William A. Byers. Another provider of funds was a "silent partner," James Fisk, who operated the Erie Railroad and had a secret arrangement with Stokes to discount freight charges for the refinery. Fisk and Stokes shared the affections of the same woman, Helen Josephine

Mansfield, and this caused animosity between the two men.

In January 1871, Fisk arranged to have Stokes arrested for embezzling funds from the refinery. He also took over the refinery by force and obtained injunctions to prevent Stokes and his mother, who owned the site, from entering the premises. The charge was dismissed and Stokes was later awarded $10,000 compensation. Stokes was dissatisfied with the award and was threatening to publish incriminating letters from Fisk unless he was paid substantially more.

Fisk obtained another injunction to prevent the publication, claiming he was being blackmailed. Soon after, Stokes found out that Fisk had indicted him for attempted blackmail with the Grand Jury. On January 6, 1872, Fisk was visiting the Grand Central Hotel, lower Broadway, when Stokes met him on the stairs and shot him twice. He died the next day.

Now the interesting part; Jim was having no participation in this fascinating scam. He absolutely refused to pay a dime. Stokes, bordering on bankruptcy confronted Jim in January 1872 in the Grand Central Hotel, shot him once in the arm and once in the stomach. Jim died the next day, age 37.

The Trial

Stokes was arrested and tried on three occasions. He claimed he shot in self-defense, and a gun later found in a sofa at the hotel gave credibility to his assertion that Fisk had a weapon. At the first trial, the jury could not agree on a verdict. The second was declared a mistrial and on the third occasion, he was found guilty of manslaughter. He was sentenced to four years and sent to Sing-Sing and later Auburn prison from where he was released in October 1876. His father had died whilst he was in prison and his wife had been taken to Europe by her father during the period of the trials.

The letters were published and contained nothing out of the ordinary, just love things that love letters usually consist of.

Twenty thousand people attended Fiske's funeral.

Stokes served four years of a six-year prison sentence in Sing Sing Penitentiary.

Cornerstone
Moral personal relationships

Jekyll Island Club and the Federal Reserve
The Millionaire's Enclave
Exclusivity was its province

The Grand Dinning Hall at Jekyll Island Club
Photo by Ron Chicone 2010

For every season a time, for every time an age, for every age a reason. Beauty is not a constant for every individual. I can only speak for myself when I speak glowingly about this island on the Georgia coast.

Please allow me to rescind that statement. This beautiful place will live in the eyes, the mind, the heart of anyone who has ever seen a majestic oak, over-flowing with Spanish moss, eyes that can behold the immense vista of marshland, teeming with the treasures of the sea, vast areas that bring the palms and the various Old South flora into spectacular view, and a mind that goes to a level of complete relaxation because of surroundings that are surreal. You have just entered the lowlands of the Deep South.

Union Club 1860

Union Club Ball Room

In this chapter, I am asking you to stay and visit for a while, and allow the ghosts that are so plentiful to invade your reverie. As you let your mind open, you will meet the extremely wealthy, the idle rich, and others who were the industrialists that made our nation into the savior of the free world.

The old New York Union Club is the second oldest gentleman's club in America, established in 1836 and the impetus of the evolution of The Jekyll Island Club. The New York Club was, by any definition, truly palatial.

Outside stairs controlled the entrance that was patrolled by security guards that generally did not require your identification; your personage was instantly recognized and you were shown into the sitting room, where the members would hold sway with whatever the political ramifications of the day were occurring. This room was generally called the B. S. room and much of it was tossed around in this venue:

Members of some note were:

- *John Jacob Astor IV – Titanic victim*
- *Dwight D. Eisenhower – President of the United States*
- *Ulysses S. Grant – Civil War General and President of the United States*
- *William Randolph Hearst – Newspapers and owner of Hearst Castle*

- *Leonard Jerome – Grandfather of Winston Churchill*
- *J. P. Morgan – Financier*
- *Winfield Scott – General of the Army*
- *Philip Sheridan – General of the Army*
- *William T. Sherman – General of the Army*
- *Cornelius Vanderbilt – Shipping and Railroads*

Many others of rather impressive pedigree attended this club. One of the noteworthy articles of faith included the fact that members who belonged to the Confederacy were never expelled or forced to give up their memberships. Consequently, these Southern members were all too familiar with the Georgia coast, and almost certainly were the go-to-guys when discussing investments regarding land to purchase when establishing hunting and fishing reserves in the South.

One of the members never included in talks about establishing a southern reserve was William Tecumseh Sherman. Even 20 years after the end of the "War Between the States," animosity still ran high among not only southern sympathizers, but also some northern members, who almost certainly had relatives living in the Confederacy and could not easily forget the scorched earth destruction visited on the South by Sherman. He was easily the most reviled survivor of that war. He did not mind being excluded, because he had no intention of returning to an area where his life could have been in danger.

The members of the Union Club had given thought to having a retreat for hunting and fishing almost from the time the New York Club was formed. After the war, the way became clearer because of reconstruction in the south. Pardon the pun, but, at this time, land was dirt-cheap. Money was not of importance; however, in the Union Club's acquiring land for the development of hunting and fishing grounds, the right piece of property was of the utmost importance. They had been casting about in all directions and not coming up with anything that caught their fancy.

One evening, as they sat in the BS room, or in the nicer parlance of the day, "The Lounge," John Pierpont Morgan was holding court as he often did, Members gave him much leeway because of his extraordinary success in matters of finance, and much influence, not only in the hierarchy of the administration in Washington, but around the world. He was a rather large and rotund man with a red, bulbous nose that was large and prominent because of rosacea. This did not detract from his commanding presence. On this evening, cigar smoke was thick in the atmosphere of the room; Morgan was conversing with a gentleman who sported a rather bushy beard, a cigar, and a jigger of bourbon on the table next to him.

"Ulysses, are you going to get on board with our project of a southern encampment?" he asked.

The eighteenth President of the United States flicked the ash of his cigar into an ashtray and responded, "I'm all for the membership of this club acquiring this thing that you have been pumping for years, but, you know Morgan, I'm getting along in years, and I do prize my comfort. In my lifetime, I've had enough roughing it, to last me until I die. So you boys have a nice time with this little project, but count me out. However, if I can be of help, you can depend on me."

A committee had been formed some time ago to pursue this project, and as yet, had not met with any success. William Cutting, estate magnate who was listening interjected.

"I know of a member who may be of some help, by the name of Newton Finney, He has some business interests in coastal Georgia. I believe he is in the billiards room playing Bottle Pool."

That particular game was one of the favorites of the Union Club. The club had recently changed its bylaws and allowed women to step into positions that were formerly held by men and the post of concierge was now held by a lovely and ingratiating woman. She immediately summoned Mr. Finney and he languidly strolled into the lounge. When asked about land that might be obtained in the south, it instantly piqued his interest.

As fate would have it, his brother in-law had recently inherited an Island on the Georgia coast called Jekyll Island that his family had owned for about 100 years.

Newton Finney   **President Grant**   **J.P. Morgan**

This timely bit of news was instantly relayed to the other members in the lounge. J. P. asked the location and was vaguely informed that it was south of Savannah. J.P. then turned to Sheridan and asked him, if he knew of anyone who was familiar with the Savannah Area. "I certainly do," Sheridan said. "I will talk to William Hardee. He was the Confederate General who opposed Sherman's march to the sea."

With that, members waited to receive further information from Finney. In the meantime, Sheridan communicated with Hardee's children (Hardee by this time had passed away) and they informed him "Jekyll Island was a prized piece of real estate that had everything the members were looking for. Finney later informed them the Island could be obtained for the rather steep price of $125,000.

A few members had private yachts, and this gave them an excuse to mount a mission to Jekyll Island, as it was then spelled, later changed to Jekyll. This mission was partly funded by the Union Club and the balance by the members themselves and it ended up being quite an armada of people, but well worth the trip.

When the armada returned and informed the members what they had encountered, their enthusiasm knew no bounds, and they immediately set about creating the documents of purpose and incorporation, with an initial 53 members that would grow to the maximum number of 100.

Purpose

"To own and maintain a hunting, fishing, yachting, and general sporting resort, to promote social intercourse among its members and their families, and to carry out such other purpose, authorized by its charter, as may be determined by the Board of Directors, Jekyll Island Club Officers, members, Constitution, Bylaws, and Charter book."

So read the words of the official charter.

An architect and construction company was hired forthwith, and construction was started in 1886, and completed in 1888. The building was an immense and beautiful structure, designed by Charles Alexander of Chicago that complemented the tastes of the Victorian era. Many problems were encountered in building this edifice, such as finding and hiring of laborers. Skilled craftsmen had to be imported from the North and building supplies transported by ship.

Its remote location necessitated building roads to the site, so the importation of horses, mules, carts and wagons had to be undertaken, along with the implements and mechanics to keep it all running smoothly. Tents and temporary housing, medical facilities, chefs, cooks and tons of food had to be imported, gardens established, and eventually, this magnificent structure arose from the heavily forested island.

The Club as it looked in the late 1800's

Today

Member's Cottage's

By the 1930's, the members considered this building hopelessly outdated, and if the money had been available would have torn it down and replaced it with what would have been considered a more modern edifice. Funny, what goes around comes around. It's now revered and considered priceless.

Buildings come and go, but this building captures the imagination, the spirit, the eternal quest that exists in all of us for a time in the past we can no longer visit, and wish we could go back in time and live in this creation just one moment in that bygone age, a time when you dressed for dinner, men wore ties to play golf, woman wore hats with a flair that no longer exists, inter-personal relationships were paramount, picnics were done with panache, "elegance surrounded everything they did". In every one of us, that glimmer of sophistication is still there.

Members matriculated to this enclave, generally, for about three or four months. The weather was exquisite in the winter months—January, February, and March were the preferred season—but many members came down in November. To northerners coming out of the cold and snow, this had to seem like heaven. Add to this the lure of hunting and fishing, tennis, golf, bicycling and many other appealing pursuits.

One other activity was carried on in the dining room, card room, poolroom, or out on the beautiful veranda; "the pursuit of money," adding to the members' many millions. This endeavor was one never talked about openly, that would have been considered the height of indiscretion. Many of the largest deals this country has ever seen were consummated at this club, including a highly secret meeting that created the Federal Reserve, the ramifications of which were, and are, felt worldwide.

Members of this club were accustomed to an existence that can only be described as high, wide, and handsome, and the club itself was not enough to satisfy their desires. The "encampment" would have to provide them with living in a way they felt would be the *least* of what they would expect if they were home. This meant they would not live in a hotel even if it was only for a few months, and it meant servants, but they never used that word, preferring "household help."

So, they went on to build what they called "cottages" on the grounds of the club, generally within walking distance of the main edifice. These cottages consisted of anywhere from 3,000 to 6,000 square feet, which gave them ample room to provide a domicile for their entire household staffs. Built in various styles; initially in the Victorian motif, which was in vogue. As time went by, other, more lavish styles, with a greater degree of opulence, were introduced, especially in the roaring '20s, when the club reached its zenith.

They soon wanted more than a bedroom to occupy, so another wing was added with 8 apartments. Later they developed an annex containing 6 apartments on 3 floors and a fourth floor for household help. This building was called the Sans Souci, meaning, in French, "without care." Some of the first residents of this addition were the Morgan's, Hyde's, and Rockefellers. Sans Souci was a misnomer when applied to these gentlemen.

In truth, the Jekyll Island Club was a great place to be employed. The majority of employees were part-timers, employed for just 3 or 4 months, and were cherry picked from prestigious establishments in the north. Staffs were more than happy to put aside all their cares, cold, snow, ice, and blizzard conditions, all travails of the frozen north. We need to remember, in that long ago time, some people were still using horses and buggies! You can only imagine what it meant to travel and luxuriate under palms, and in your off hours, to put a worm on a hook and savor the ocean and tidal basin where abundance seemed to be your right. If their northern employers gave them a problem with leaving for 3 or 4 months, usually a visit from one of the New York Union Club members could alleviate it.

The full-time staff was treated very well by the Jekyll Club superintendents and Club officers. Everything in the way of making life as pleasant as possible for the staff was provided for, including churches, medical care, out-of-the-ordinary housing, after-hour's recreation, and use of the facilities that were normally only available to the members. The golf course was a case in point: members four months, employee's *eight* months. This policy was also extended to African-Americans; certain mores of segregation still existed here, but were trivialized to a great extent. Jekyll staff members were quite progressive for the time and locale. Surprisingly, there was very little discrimination shown, even though this Island was situated in the Deep South.

Nevertheless, even in this dreamland, certain aspects of life could not be left behind.

Accidents still happened, drownings; accidental shootings while hunting, even vehicular crashes, which seems odd given the dearth of traffic on the Island. However, most deaths occurred because of sickness, disease, or old age.

Joseph Pulitzer

One death that was particularly poignant happened to a member, "Joseph Pulitzer," held in high esteem by most members, but in others, evoked a measure of fear. He owned newspapers, namely the *New York World*, where he became the champion of the common man, with exposés and a hard-hitting, populist approach. He eventually shifted his focus to human-interest stories, scandal, and sensationalism. At one point in his career; 1909, the *World* exposed an illegal payment of $40,000,000 to the French Panama Canal Co. Pulitzer was indicted for libeling President Theodore Roosevelt, and J. P. Morgan, the courts dismissed the indictment.

In 1887, the *World* introduced the first immensely popular comic strip in color, "The Yellow Kid."

Henceforth, the term "Yellow Journalism" came into vogue and is routinely used today.

Anti-Semitism was alive and well in the country at this time, and Pulitzer was attacked in print as "Judas Pulitzer." Accolades are due the Jekyll Island Club for its forbearance of an anti-Semitic stand. If there was anti-Semitism, it was underground and only whispered in hushed tones. As a matter of fact, Pulitzer had sacked many of his friends at the club, but they never held it against him.

Pulitzer dearly loved Jekyll and generally beat the other members in taking up residence; November was his preferred time of arrival. He suffered many ailments, and as his time on this earth drew to a close, he expressed the wish that he could die at Jekyll. On October 1911, he boarded his highly prized yacht, Liberty, and in failing health, started the journey to his beloved Jekyll. He made it as far as Charleston Harbor, but, on October 29, he passed away, never having made it to the one spot he loved most of all.

In the voyage through life, as happens to all, "the journey is never quite complete."

The Federal Reserve

Creation of the Federal Reserve, November 1910

Here is truly an earth-shattering event that changed the way business was conducted in this country. Much controversy took place over this event, primarily because people felt too much power was being placed in this creation and taken away from the constitutionally-elected Congress, where the purse strings of the country were properly controlled, and given to twelve large banks, which allowed them to create money without the authorization of Congress.

In order to get this underway, it had to be done in great secrecy, so the populace would not be informed until the deed was done, fearing, if word got out, it would be squashed by Congress or a popular uprising of the people. Safety of the participants was another concern. About one third of the wealth of the world was represented there. They pulled it off smoothly, the press was never the wiser, and here is how this whole thing became reality on Jekyll Island.

Forbes magazine founder, Bertie Charles Forbes wrote several years later:

"Picture a party of the nation's greatest bankers stealing out of New York on a private railroad car under cover of darkness, stealthily riding hundreds of miles south, embarking on a mysterious launch, sneaking onto an island deserted by all but a few servants, living there a full week under such rigid secrecy that the names of not one of them was once mentioned, lest the servants learn the identity and disclose to the world this strangest, most secret expedition in the history of American finance.

I am not romancing; I am giving to the world, for the first time, the real story of how the famous Aldrich Currency Report, the foundation of our new currency system, was written.

The utmost secrecy was enjoined upon all. "The public must not glean a hint of what is to be done." Senator Aldrich notified each one to go quietly into a private car, of which the railroad had received orders to draw up on an unfrequented platform. Off the party set, New York's ubiquitous reporters had been foiled. Nelson (Aldrich) had confided to Henry, Frank, Paul and Piatt that he was to keep them locked up at Jekyll Island, out of the rest of the world, until they had evolved and compiled a scientific currency system for the United States, the real birth of the present Federal Reserve System, the plan done on Jekyll Island in the conference with Paul, Frank and Henry …. Warburg is the link that binds the Aldrich system and the present system together. He, more than any one man, has made the system possible as a working reality.

Now, imagine if you can the overriding reason for the Federal Reserve to exist. It was to keep the banks from exceeding normal boundaries and exercise due diligence when lending or investing in derivatives or other securities that may be tainted.

A short explanation of derivatives is an investment in a security that is an intangible. Given the power the Fed has, one has to wonder where the Fed was hiding in 2007 and 2008. Not mine to question why, mine to do or die or, at the very least lose my money without whimpering.

The Federal Reserve Act was finally passed in the fall of 1913. It was based on the final edicts of Senator Nelson Aldrich, a member of the Jekyll Island Club and sponsored by Carter Glass and Robert Owen and became known as the Glass-Owen Bill.

President Woodrow and Edith Wilson

Another event of some note that took place at Jekyll Island was the visit of President Woodrow Wilson in 1915. The Club was all-atwitter over this and everyone wanted to make this a memorable stop for the highest officer of the land, so they outdid themselves.

As the President's yacht hove into view, they released an impressive display of fireworks and canon. When the President and the First Lady disembarked from a smaller sloop and stepped onto the pier, a ten-gun salute was fired by Military Reservists obtained from Brunswick, Georgia. Appropriate Flags and Bunting lined the path to the Club. It was a gala affair in the dining room and ballroom that evening. Waltzes by a string quartet gave just the right tone to the whole event. Edith Galt Wilson, the First Lady, was at first prepared to be bored on one of the innumerable trips required of sitting Presidents.

Once she was mesmerized by the paradigm of an example that existed only on this Island, and was wined, dined and feted by the extraordinary gentleman of this very unique club, her attitude did a complete turnaround. That evening was one, in later years, she would reminisce about.

World War I was now underway in Europe, and our country was entering a period of deep concern for our boys, who would be embarking for the continent and dying in some God-forsaken foxhole or trench. It would be a long time before we, as a nation would rise with our heads up and see a brighter future. World War II would be the final cataclysmic event that would write the last chapter of the Jekyll Island Club.

The many good things that happened at this club were interspersed with tragedy, but none more tragic then the eventual demise of the life and times of not only this club, but of America. The 1920s was truly the time to be a member of Jekyll. The financial markets were soaring and businesses were roaring. After all, it was called "The Roaring '20s" and everybody had untold resources. Credit was readily available, securities were bought with 10% down on the dollar and millionaires were literally made overnight. President Hoover proclaimed "two chickens in every pot, two cars in every garage." People partied away the night doing the dances of the age, the Charleston, the Big Apple, the Black Bottom, Jitterbug was now making an appearance, woman were smoking in public and styles that woman wore enhanced sexuality.

Finally, 1929 came and the party was over. It came to an end with a crash and a gigantic hangover as most parties do. The club began to reel under the crushing weight of expenses and declining memberships. Former millionaires were going into bankruptcy and literally walking out on their beautiful Jekyll Island homes, totally abandoning them, and taking nothing, leaving even their furniture behind.

The club cast about in desperation for ways to save itself. Memberships were expanded and fees lowered, which was self-defeating, because there were no members to be found at any price.

Whenever you think things cannot get any worse, of course they will. A double whammy hit and World War II became a reality. All of our industry converted to war materials.

Ford, General Motors, and others were now making tanks. Henry Kaiser was building Liberty Ships and became known for his fast production methods. Rationing was the rage. Whenever you saw a line forming, you got in it, and whatever they were providing, you needed it.

The most critical shortage was men. The draft sucked away most of the men, depleting the labor supply. This put the final nail in the coffin of the Jekyll Club, and after heroic efforts to keep the Club alive, it was closed at the end of the 1942 season.

There was a glimmer of hope that the Club would become viable again after the war, but this hope faded and the Club became a ward of the State of Georgia in 1947, when the entire island was purchased by the State Government.

The state tried operating the entire complex as a resort, but, financially, it was a failure and closed again in 1971. It was designated as an historic landmark in 1978.

The 1930's sucked the life out of, not only The Jekyll Island Club, but the country too. If we include inflation, it took 40 years just to return to where we were financially in 1929.

As sad as it is to think about the demise of this picturesque and exquisite piece of history, there is an upside to this continuing story. We must remember this had been a place that the average person would never get to see, and to walk about the magic of its tree-lined lanes, or rent a bike and cruise around as they did in 1898. Now, that is possible because of its latest reincarnation as a luxury resort hotel. Restoration was begun in 1985 and it was reopened as an opulent resort.

If you desire to return for a brief moment to the past, then grab your suitcase and your credit card or checkbook and shuffle off to Jekyll Island.

Jessie Livermore

$Jesse Livermore$
The Great Bear of Wall Street

At the end of this chapter, I will reveal the secret that was the source of Jesse Livermore earning many millions in the stock market and the mystery that contributed to his eventual demise.

Jesse Livermore, That name will live in the annals of fame wherever men of intellect gather to discuss investments and winning and losing on that great street called Wall Street, names that can be mentioned in the same breath, Bernard Baruch, J. P. Morgan, Billy Durant, John D. Rockefeller, Joe Kennedy, Richard Whitney and many others that became legendary.

Most of the great speculators made much of their fortunes from the bull market of the 1920s. We came to refer to that time as the Roaring '20s. A time that, for many of us, held a fascination because of America breaking away from a traditionalist and conservative way of life to an avant-garde lifestyle. It was the heyday of prohibition, speakeasies, gangsters, flappers, dances that were fast and provocative like the Charleston, the Black Bottom, the Big Apple, the beginning of the Jitterbug.

Women were suddenly free to become a part of life they never before experienced. They now smoked in the open, drank booze in the open, adhered to contemporary styles of dress that clearly showed a new sexuality, with hairstyles that were a significant departure from the past.

The Start of the Great Depression

On black Thursday, October 24, 1929, the stock market started falling precipitously at the opening bell. This was the clarion call for the bankers, and movers and shakers to hold a meeting and essentially do what they formerly did to stop a market panic in 1907. The meeting included, Thomas W. Lamont, acting head of Morgan Bank; Albert Wiggin, head of the Chase National Bank and Charles G. Mitchell, President of the National City Bank of New York. Richard Whitney, Vice President of the New York

Exchange, who later would become president of the Exchange, and end up in prison for misappropriation. A nice word for embezzlement. Richard became the front man for this illustrious group, the man they forgot about and the one that was the driving force in the 1907 debacle of the securities market was Jesse Livermore.

Jesse was involved in selling prodigious amounts of stock short, a powerful mechanism for driving stock prices down. It involved borrowing shares and selling them immediately with the intention of buying the security back at some future date and replacing it at a lower price. Of course, this just fed upon itself. The more it went down the more sellers entered the market and the more it went down. And round and round it went.

October 29, 1929, Black Tuesday
The day the Roaring '20s ended.

At this point, I believe I must explain in more detail what a short sale is. It occurs when a speculator borrows stock from his broker and immediately sells it to take advantage of the current price and hopefully buy it back at a lower price, and replace the shares that he borrowed.

Let's say that GM stock is selling at 100 and the speculator believes that GM stock will decline. He will borrow the number of shares that he wants to sell and get the price that it is selling at currently. If GM declines to 90 or any amount below the price he sold it at, he can buy it back and replace the borrowed stock. At $90, he will make a ten-dollar profit. Let's further assume that margin is 10-percent, which means he borrows 90-percent, and let me interject here, a 10-percent margin is not in the cards in the present day. Currently it is 50-percent. Now, he sells 1000 shares, and the cost of shares if he had bought them would have been $100,000. But he needed to put up only $10,000. If he made a return of $10 a share, his profit is $10,000 or a percentage return of 100%. If you can understand all that, you are now an expert and can now make millions in the market.

Of course, I was being facetious, but can you see why many people felt that way? You watched your neighbor scrape together $1000 and make three or four thousand before the month was out, not by selling short but buying long. Long in this context meant actually buying and owning a security.

There was a general feeling at that time that the market had reached a new level and would only go up from here. This Pollyanna view was promoted by reporters, pseudo financial experts and other market pundits of the day.

History does repeat itself. Haven't we heard the siren song of that old refrain just about every time we are in an exalted bull market? Of course, the lemmings enter at about this time and guess who ends up on the short end of the stick?

Panic of 1907   **Crash 1929**

In the foregoing, I refer to the lemmings as the small, uninformed investor, but Jesse was not just a prolific short seller; he simply went with the market. By tape reading, he could divine whether the market, in its entirety, was headed in an upward or downward direction. Once that was determined, then, and only then, he would select a stock and either bet it short or long. By looking closely at the volume and momentum of a security, he could tell in many cases which way the momentum of the issue was headed.

We must remember his trading system was not as simplified as the foregoing indicates. Many long hours, days, and years were involved in the building of Jesse's system. By getting a feel for this 1929 market during the course of the year, he determined that it was vastly overpriced.

During the summer, he started shorting the market, but the securities he shorted kept going up, which of course was the wrong direction. If Jesse had one virtue, it was patience. He was absolutely positive this market was overpriced, and it was just a matter of time before the break came. Come it did ... with a vengeance. It is generally believed that the selling climaxed on October 29 when new records of volume were set. However the securities markets continued down until the Second World War started, a total of about 10 years. Taking inflation into consideration, it took a total of 40 years for the market to get back to where it was at its height in the fateful year of 1929.

Shorting the market in this horrendous period of time, Jesse reached the peak of his life as far as his fortune was concerned. He earned in 1929 approximately

100 million dollars of course, you can only imagine what that meant during the 30's.

Yes, the Roaring Twenties ended, but with a roaring, unimaginable crash that hopefully we will never see again. A philosopher once said, *"If we forget history, we are doomed to repeat it."* This, then, was a time of suicides. It was widely reported that men were jumping out of high-rise buildings. It was also a time of soup lines, men, women and children, living on the street, or in bushes, or abandoned buildings, or patched tents and ramshackle structures put together with grocery boxes that at one time held oranges or apples. People were begging for anything they could get, food, money, a job, whatever was offered. The poverty and suffering was unimaginable and it extended to the entire U. S.

Farmers actually were hit with this downturn more than the city dwellers, hit with a double whammy when the great dust storms came along in the '30s, and the massive migration to California and the western U. S. began. Have you ever heard of the term Okies? That's what they were called. Hatred was rampant among the permanent residents they were displacing. One can only imagine the despair they were all feeling.

Jesse was the most hated man on Wall Street, because of his predilection of selling stocks which tended to drive the market in the wrong direction, *down*. This sentiment included President Herbert Hoover; whom the populace put the blame on for the Great Depression.

It therefore became incumbent on Jesse to protect his family. Answering his phone was not an option, because of the venom that was spewed out when he did answer it. Bodyguards were hired to protect his wife and children, and various mansions that contained many beautiful antiques, paintings and other possessions, were closely guarded.

Jesse started at the tender age of 14 as a chalkboard boy, in a firm called Paine Webber. This came about after he ran away from home, but with the encouragement of his mother, who realized he did not belong on a hardscrabble farm etching a living out of an unforgiving, stone-filled patch of dirt.

Jesse was an exceedingly bright young man with a penchant for mathematics. Having landed this job as a chalkboard boy, he undoubtedly felt it was the job of his dreams. He loved being The constant hammering of the ticker tape, the brokers yelling out orders, the names of the companies on the board, with changing numbers every second, men winning and losing thousands of dollars in every change of the numbers was like candy to young Jesse and his appetite for it knew no bounds.

The things he learned there would stand him in good stead in later years, the basis for the system of trading he eventually developed. It was called "tape reading," in other words, getting a feel for the market or a particular stock. He began to realize that these numbers ran in a pattern and could be predictable. His affinity for numbers would be the basis for his ability to accumulate the many millions of dollars this talent created for him.

You would think that with his keen, mathematical background, he would have a conservative bent, but that wasn't the case at all. He was a plunger, and he became known as the "boy plunger of Wall Street." This led to his being broke, losing everything he had, not once, not twice, but many times. In fact, so many times he lost track.

So, you see, it wasn't the money, like many of the outstanding men and women of our time, and in times past, it was "the game," the money only a way of knowing if you were winning or losing.

The panic of 1907 was a loan driven, market downturn. Every day at noon bankers would appear at the posts of the Stock Exchange and announce to the brokers how much call money they had to offer. Call money was the funds that the brokers made available to their customers so they would have margin to buy stocks. This was the grease that made the brokers and some customers wealthy. The banks suddenly ran out of money. This happened because the brokers had become overextended.

If money was not obtainable, then it follows that the amount of stock sold and bartered on the exchange would show a precipitous decline. Hence, a crash would be in the offing. Then, as now, everybody needed the availability of liquid money from sources that supplied the loans, banks, insurance companies, etc. This was one of the factors that contributed to every crash that we have experienced in our history, including our recent steep declines, i.e. 1987 and 2008.

The question becomes; do we currently have circuit breakers in place to blunt a steep decline in the market? That is worrisome, considering the speed of trading in our modern, electronically driven era.

Back in 1907, a market decline would be blunted by a consortium of immensely wealthy men and entities, which would supply enough muscle, and by that I mean, money to start buying stocks in enough volume to halt the decline. That tactic can't work today. The sheer size of our interconnected markets would preclude this particular method from being effective.

J. P. Morgan

When it came to the attention of J. P. Morgan that a problem was developing in the market, he sent one of his men to the exchange to tell them that call money would be there at the opening of the market. He summoned the banks and ordered them to make call money available immediately. When they asked where they would get the money, he replied, "They should raid their reserves." The banks replied, "We will be in violation of banking codes." Morgan said, "I'll personally guarantee your reserves. If there are other problems with government edicts I will personally deal with them and back everything you do with the entire Morgan organization.

More than that, he gathered many of the most powerful men in the country to start buying some of the most high-profile stocks.

J. P., being a wise man, knew what most people on Wall Street did not, that Jesse Livermore would be the most prolific short seller on the street, contributing to the sliding prices of stocks. He knew that in order to halt the slippery slope, he must enlist his participation. With all due swiftness, he sent an emissary to speak to J. L. as he liked to be called. Jesse had never been sought out by a man as powerful as J. P. Morgan, and he was duly flattered. Jesse did not have an ego and did not consider himself as having much in the way of power in the overall market, but he quickly complied when Morgan asked him to curtail operations.

The next morning, he immediately covered his shorts, went long in some high volume companies and the panic of 1907 was averted. However, his intervention by going long in the market cost Jesse dearly. This then, was the thing that made him strengthen his resolve. He would never again listen to another person, or be overcome and impressed by another's fame or importance.

Never take a tip or insider information. Never let his ego interfere with the business of making money. Always go it alone. These were his credos, but, because of human frailty, he did violate this rule once or twice, and each time, it cost him lost time and money.

Jesse was the personification of the Roaring 20's. Slim, blond, pale blue eyes, very much a meticulous dresser, he had a tendency to be flamboyant. He had several mansions properly staffed with butlers and maids, not to mention yachts that reached upwards of 300 feet and properly staffed. This was in keeping with his personality. Everything about him was orderly and neat, something that extended into his entire life. He arose at the same time, ate at the same time, and had his chauffeur and Rolls Royce bring him to his palatial and regal office at the same time. Order did not always extend to trading activities. He was primarily a tape reader; however, he could be impetuous and spontaneous. He never took, or listened to, tips or inside information. The few times he did, had disastrous consequences.

One particular occurrence did not meet with an undue loss of capital. It seems Jesse had an unreal clairvoyance and feel for things that might happen in the future that would have an effect on his trading. For instance, he decided to sell short Union Pacific Railroad for no known reason, two days before the disastrous San Francisco earthquake hit, and literally made him a fortune when the bottom fell out of Union Pacific stock.

The following is the one time that J. L. did not follow his rules of the game, much to his chagrin, and it led to his eventual bankruptcy. On one of Jesse's many excursions to Palm Beach, which he found wondrous in the richness of its population, the beauty of its mansions and the verdant nature of its environs, he was enjoying himself in the exquisite confines of the most celebrated casino of its day, called Bradley's Beach Club.

Sitting at the bar, with Lillian Russell, the most alluring actress and singer of the day, and Edward Bradley, the proprietor of the establishment, a gentleman by the name of Percy Thomas entered. Known as the cotton king, it was a well-known fact he had a wealth of knowledge in the commodities market. Suave, smooth, self-assured and a persona that could only be called enigmatic, he was the complete opposite of J. L. Where Jesse tended to be withdrawn and taciturn, Thomas was open, loquacious, and personable.

Jessie operated alone, without inside information or, many times, without any information at all. Remember, he was a tape reader and acted only on the information the tape gave him. But Percy had an all-encompassing knowledge and many spies working for him. He had acquired, through the force of his personality, many people who were in positions to enable him to acquire knowledge of privileged situations. Only after his information was complete, would he purchase a position in that particular investment.

J. L. and Percy eventually established an exceptionally close bond and Jesse started believing that the way Percy speculated was the perfect way to trade. One time in the past the cotton king had gone broke. Jesse always had the ability to coldly analyze any situation and now this happenstance weighed on Jesse's mind. How could Percy go broke if he knew everything?

Regardless of his haunting suspicions, Jesse was eventually hooked. He had an uncommonly bright, inquiring mind and all of the frailties of a human being. He thought there was always a better way to do things. All of the lessons he had learned in many years of trading were put aside. This had to be a better way because all the information that Percy had accumulated said so. Yet, he forgot the most powerful lesson of all. *The market seldom does what you think it ought to do.*

The other valuable lesson? *Trade by yourself and keep your own counsel.* Jesse was now playing another man's game and it was a time of impending disasters that meant bankruptcy for Jesse.

Lillian Russell was the first to go. He found her high maintenance ways too rich for his new position in life, so he sent her back to Diamond Jim Brady, a former companion of hers. He was an extremely corpulent man, who had a fascination for diamonds and could well afford them. Owning and doing many things, Diamond Jim was a successful and controversial businessman, known to be somewhat unethical. We're not sure if Diamond Jim knew that Lillian was spending time with other men, or if he even cared. Lillian believed the size of a man's waist was of no concern, but the size of his wallet was immensely influential to her.

The second thing to go was his yacht, his beloved *Anita Venetian*, and one by one, the estates were liquidated and he pawned the many jewels' his wife had accumulated.

Jesse was now back in an environment that he was all too familiar with. Slammed to earth with a thud that made waves throughout Wall Street and with hat in hand, J. L. went visiting all of the old brokers he had done business with in the past. They had persevered with him in other times, and this time was no different. They rushed to his side and made margin available to him so he could start trading again and it did not take long for Jesse to start acquiring his former status.

There was a price to be paid, however. A hole was left in Jesse's persona. Some of the cocksure stride was gone, and many times, he found himself trading without conviction. This hampered his formula for success and increased his many moods of depression. Possibly, he became bipolar or manic-depressive. This condition would last the rest of his life. He was not getting the pleasure that he had previously experienced in the times when he was winning large amounts of money.

Ziegfeld Follies—Jesse's wife—Dorothy

The one thing that stayed with him was his attraction for the opposite sex. He for them and them for him. Always a handsome man, he loved beautiful ladies. As a matter of fact, F. Scott Fitzgerald, who created the phrase The Roaring Twenties, probably used Jesse as his model for Gatsby when writing his best-selling, wildly popular book, *The Great Gatsby*. I believe that Fitzgerald and J. L. were friends and had been to many of the parties that Jesse's Ziegfeld Follies second wife, Dorothy, sponsored. Both Fitzgerald and Dorothy were alcoholics, so there was somewhat of a bond infused into this relationship.

The drinking and loose morals of the rich and famous, or infamous, whichever way you want to term it, was the beginning of the final chapter of the Jesse Livermore saga. Here, the degradation and dissipation take place. It is difficult to pin the entire blame on either party. Certainly, there was enough to go around. Jesse had his amorous ways and thirst for beautiful showgirls. Dorothy had her thirst for the demon rum. This led Dorothy to have numerous affairs, especially since she was living with a man who spent most of his time being morose and in a deep dark funk and seemingly did not care about his wife or children. He, however had to come home to an alcoholic and

those of you who ever had to live with a person whose only reason for living was to get to the next drink, know how absolutely disgusting this can be and how repulsive they are in their personal habits and with alcoholic friends swarming around them.

When they divorced in 1932, I believe it was the end for Jesse. He still carried a torch for her, but they just could not be together. She knew of his extra-marital affairs, and that tore at her heart. Of course, she started having her own dalliances and eventually a nasty split took place over the children. She eventually won custody, and J. L. took it hard. It was difficult for him to understand how two very privileged boys could be brought up in an atmosphere of alcoholism.

He did provide her with a generous settlement as he did with his first wife. Believing he would make it up in a short while, as he was able to do all of his life. A short list of what he gave her follows:

- A one-million-dollar portfolio of stocks hand-picked by Jesse,
- A beautiful awe-inspiring estate that was the envy of her many friends and was used by Fitzgerald as the model of the mansion in his book The Great Gatsby
- All the exquisite furnishings, including Louie the XIV furnishings
- Tons of silverware, including the Napoleon serving set for sixteen.
- Several beautiful cars, including a Rolls Royce.
- Persian rugs.

- Drapes and window dressings that Scarlet O'Hara would have married Rhett for.
- The interior of the mansion had been appointed by the exceptional decorators of the day.

After the divorce in the courthouse, she immediately walked into another courtroom and married a man by the name of Walter Longcope, a tax collector, a handsome man, but who certainly had never known money like Dorothy had. This too ended in divorce.

The first thing that left Dorothy's possession was Jesse's handpicked stock portfolio. Under the advice of a Financial Advisor of the day, who told her that railroad bonds with their attractive dividends would give her a lovely annual income? This is the same advice that we receive from present day Advisors, whose mantra is mutual funds, bonds, or annuities. Eventually, her railroad bonds became worthless. If she had kept the handpicked portfolio by J. L., it would have been worth 50 million by 1950.

She eventually moved into the mansion *Evermore*. She took her two dogs with her, and while she lolled around in a drunken haze, she never took the dogs out onto the expansive and expensive grounds. They proceeded to urinate and defecate on the beautiful Persian rugs, and when the rugs were too foul and the stench unbearable, she just rolled them up and threw them out.

The Louie XIV furniture was so badly mistreated, to say they were junk would have been upgrading them to an unattainable status. When the taxman presented her a bill on the home, she sent it on to Jesse, whom he promptly ignored and the home was foreclosed on.

The cost of the antique furniture was in the millions. The home was appraised in 1932 at $1,350,000, the landscaping at $150,000, the silverware at $100,000, a Rolls Royce at $22,000 and jade ornaments at $300,000. The entire ensemble, auctioned, hammer down at $250,000.

Jesse remarried eight months later to a socialite, Harriet Metz Noble of Omaha, Nebraska, from a wealthy family that owned the Metz Brewery in Omaha. Harriet was an Opera singer and with her résumé came a truly ominous sign. This shows the depths that the once well-respected speculator had reached. She had been married four previous times. That's bad enough, but can you imagine a man, reputed to have a brilliant mind, after what he had been through, marrying a woman who's four previous husbands committed suicide. "Whoa, wait a minute!" Jesse should have given this more than a passing thought.

I believe that this woman was a very controlling person and Jesse was at a point in his life that existence held no interest for him. In other words, he allowed her to dictate his life and he proceeded to follow her around like a little puppy dog. This was so unlike Jesse. No longer did vivacity and excitement exist in his way of life. Events would later occur that were catastrophic to Jesse.

He hardly saw his two boys, Jesse, Jr. and Paul anymore because they were off at school and Dorothy's hatred for J. L. made it difficult for him to see them. Nevertheless, he loved them with all of his heart. He may not have physically seen them, but Daddy was always there when they needed anything. The one thing they needed more than anything else was his presence and counsel, something which he was incapable of giving.

Jesse Jr. a young man who was endowed with the good looks of his parents, was now becoming a problem for Dorothy, as many of her erstwhile lady friends became enamored of his looks and charms, though they were much older. They found having an afternoon tryst with this attractive young man enticing, and of course, he liked what alcohol did to him. Paul, the younger son, was certainly more sober in his appreciation of life and eventually had a small career in movies.

An evening when all combatants were inebriated, Jesse, Jr. started having a heated argument with his mother, probably over any number of things that people in their cups insanely argue about. Junior ran upstairs to grab a rifle, brought it downstairs to his mother, and handed it to her.

"You always wanted to do this," he said, "so here is your chance, shoot me."

Dorothy, in a drunken stupor, took him up on his challenge and pulled the trigger on a rifle that she thought was just a ruse. What she thought was an empty weapon, fired, and hit Jesse in the chest. In slurred words, she started screaming. "Oh, my God! I've shot my son!" she cried, over and over again.

She eventually collapsed on the floor. Other people who were there called an ambulance and Jesse Jr., still alive, was taken to the emergency room. J. L. was promptly notified and rushed to the hospital where, upon seeing his son grabbed his hand. "Fight, Jess, fight as hard as you can!" he said in despair. And fight he did, eventually surviving this traumatic event, after many prayers from J. L. and Dorothy.

The bitterness deepened between the two of them, but, when J. L. walked away, he knew the time he would spend with his family was growing short. He was already planning his final exit.

Everything was finalizing, all of the various lawsuits that were happening. His ex-wife was suing him for the hospital bills that they were charging for his son.

The Federal Government was suing for back taxes. Other people were suing just to get a piece of the fast disappearing fortune that was left, any spare change that they could get their grimy gritty hands on. These were the vultures that appeared whenever someone was down, and they thought an opportunity to feed on the bones of a decaying carcass presented itself.

Jesse was now incapable of trading like days of yore. Depression had completely engulfed him. For so many years, all of his adult life, the only thing he knew, the stock market, was now useless to him. He felt no need to go on living. Death would be a welcome respite from the terrible pain he now felt every waking moment.

J. L. and his son Paul did collaborate on a book in 1940 called, *How to Trade in Stocks*. This was an exercise in futility. At this time, J. L. certainly had remarkably little idea of how to trade in stocks, and the book sold inadequately. It has become more popular now than it was then.

On Wednesday November 27, 1940, Jesse and his wife went to one of their favorite places, the Stork Club. Jesse only picked at his food and seemed rather distant, with a faraway look in his eye. His wife, Harriet asked if there was anything wrong. He replied, he had a feeling of tiredness, so they made their goodbyes to their friend Sherman Billingsley the owner of the Stork Club, and departed rather early.

He committed suicide the next day

The next morning, on Thursday November 28, 1940, J. L. went to his office in the Squibb Building as usual and later left to go to the Sherry Netherland Hotel. He had at one time lived here and still knew a few people. It was customary for Jesse to stop here and have a cocktail when leaving his office for the day. He briefly talked to the manager and then walked into the bar, where the bartender made his usual Old Fashioned.

As he sat having lunch, he occasionally entered something on a small pad and then placed it in his pocket. The bartender thought he seemed distraught and uptight. He finally rose from the table and walked toward the banquet area and then to a cloakroom just off the ballroom. He sat on a stool, pulled a .32-cal. automatic from his pocket, calmly shot himself behind his right ear and died instantly. The notes on the pad in his pocket, as disclosed by the police, took the form of a suicide note:

My dear Nina; Things have gotten bad with me. I'm tired of fighting. Can't carry on any longer. This is the only way out. I am unworthy of your love. I am a failure. I am truly sorry, but this is the only way out for me.

There may have been more to his last words, but nothing further was ever disclosed.

The crassness of people never ceases to amaze me. Jesse's son Paul hurried over to Jesse's home to give some solace to the new widow. She apparently didn't need it. She was too busy carrying out bags full of money that Jesse kept in the apartment to foil the many people that had designs on what was left of his wealth.

As Paul watched, she went to the safe and scraped out the many jewels they had accumulated, carried them out to the waiting chauffer, and made her goodbyes to Paul.

And so ended a life that had everything: intelligence, richness, many friends, loves, success, fame, and failure. What a shame it ended as it did, the life of one of the last men to have experienced the thrill of the *Gilded Age*.

As I wrote this chapter, I felt deeply the emptiness of its ending and the termination of this special life. Only one question remains. *Why?*

Trading Secrets of Jesse Lauriston Livermore

My own experience in trading securities rivals Jesse's in the length of time that I spent in the business. I learned to read financial pages of the newspaper at about nine years old. My father, an immigrant from Italy, only had a fourth grade education. The inability to speak English with any degree of clarity was the reason he was still in the fourth grade when he quit school to go to work.

Living in Hubbard, Ohio, there seemed to be a plethora of jobs in the steel industry. He lied about his age, but, in those days, that was not a problem. If you were big enough, and willing to hold up your end of the job in the blast furnaces, your employers were happy and would not challenge your age credentials. During that time period, this was a horrendous job, since they had none of the safety precautions that are common today.

My father's belief in the American system grew stronger as time went on. Yes, he did suffer through the depression and I was old enough to remember when he had to go on relief simply to provide for the family. The men in the family would get up in the dark of the night to go to the train yards where they would hope to find coal that had fallen from the trains as they passed, and they were not above giving the coal a little help in falling from the coal cars.

At that time, the railroads employed security guards that were instructed to shoot at people who dared to breach the confines of the railroad yards. I don't know if they meant to shoot directly at them or just enough to scare the bee-*jesses* out of them. They were given the popular name, *Son-of- a- Bitch Railroad Dicks*.

To keep the lights on in our home, meant working for the utility company four days a month. Many times working sixteen hours a day. The mode of transportation to and from work was open dump trucks regardless of the weather.

The Roosevelt administration eventually started a program called the Works Progress Administration, or WPA for short, and halleluiah, my father had a job. Not much of one, but one in which you went to work every day. The ability to use a shovel was the main requirement to work on the WPA and they even paid you; not much, but, by God, it was a paycheck.

Times did get better when my father was able to land a job with General Motors. That's where the realization that he could become an owner of the company by buying stock on the stock exchange took place. His experience working for General Motors gave him the belief that this company would become richer as time went on. My dad became a part of the American dream by becoming a stockholder in the General Motors Company.

Because I showed an interest in stocks, he let me tag along with his excursions to a Paine Webber or a Merrill Lynch brokerage office. These were located on the public square in Youngstown, Ohio. Time has dimmed my memory somewhat, but I, like Jesse, was fascinated by the big board and the flashing numbers and symbols. My father, formerly a language handicapped immigrant, eventually taught me the rudiments of reading the financial pages. In time I became a Financial Advisor and retired after a career of over 30 years.

Now, following that long soliloquy, we finally come to the reason I might have a unique ability to analyze the trading systems of Jesse Livermore. First of all, is Jesse's system out of date? Not by a long shot, the difference is his approach to trading has come into the mainstream. What he called tape reading, we call charting. What took him hours or days to divine from tape reading, we do in a matter of seconds with computers.

Insider trading is given to us almost immediately; what would have taken days to determine back then. News on a security is generally instantaneous, but not always. In this day and age, our tape is always running current, not lagging behind. Sometimes it was hours behind in Jesse's day.

To get an execution on one's trade in today's world is a matter of a few seconds. The cost of making a trade is much less today, hence the advent of the day trader. That would have been anathema in Jesse's day because of costs involved. Yet, the basic premise is still the same:

1) Determine the momentum of the general securities market. There are three kinds of movements that involve securities, Up, Down, Sideways.
2) Make a determination of the sectors that are reacting in the same direction as the general market.
3) Make a determination of the securities that are reacting in the same direction as the general market.
4) If a market is going in a sideways direction, Jesse would generally stay out of the market unless the tapes would be indicating through the volume and chart/tape pattern, that a general turn in this security was indicated.
5) Never take advice from other people.
6) Never yield to insider information

7) Do yourself a favor and be a lone wolf.
8) Volume, volume, volume, was Jesse's big obsession and for an excellent reason.
9) Volume was able to tell Jesse if a security was going up or down or getting ready for a transitional turn.
10) Remember, the market is more of an art than a science.
11) Learning to have a feel for the market, or security, is of overriding importance.
12) As you mature in your trading methods, volume will become more important to you and to your ability to beat the market.

Examples:

a) Stock that is riding higher on decreasing volume is probably going to start trending the other way, or getting ready to stagnate.
b) Stock that is trending higher on incremental increases in volume will, in all likelihood, go higher.
c) The reverse may be true. A stock that is going lower on incremental increases in volume is more likely going to go lower.
d) Here is the catch. If a security has a sudden spike along with an increase in volume, either up or down in its trend, then that is what is called an exhaustion spike,

or peak, and that security will now generally take a turn either up or down. The reason is that it has exhausted either the buyers or sellers in that security.

e) Notice that, in all cases, I have referred to the various different movements in a security with a connotation such as, generally, more than likely, probably, likelihood, or maybe. The reason, the market has a peculiar way of reacting and having a mind of its own. Jesse only tried to put the prevailing odds in his favor.

13) Remember, being right all the time is impossible. The goal is being right 60% of the time.

14) Jesse, in most cases, liked to test a security before making a decisive move and he would invest small amounts. If the investment moved in the proper direction with strength, meaning volume and satisfactory movement of the price, either up or down, it would finally give him the conviction that he was correct in his assessment of that investment and he now would make a much larger outlay of capital.

15) Never allow a loss of greater than 10%. A favorite homily of mine that falls in the same category: Never fall in love with any investment because it will never love you back.

16) Absolutely do not listen to other investors that will try to tell you how truly great they are doing in the market. Always treat them as prevaricators and never allow dreams of sugarplums to dance in your head.

I must give my impressions of the real reason that Jesse eventually failed in the final days of his career. Of course I will also point out that many other successful traders failed in the '30s. Why, all of a sudden, did nothing go right for them? It was because of the quirky nature of the market in that period of time. Their previous experiences taught them that markets always righted themselves. That had been so right through most of the time there were security markets.

I'm sure you have heard of long term investing? Keeping and holding quality stocks over the long term. There are many market mavens who espouse that same rhetoric today, and mostly, they are right. But, occasionally, they are wrong with disaster lurking around the corner. This is where Jesse's 10% rule came into play. When a stock went against him ten percent, he would cover his positions, and terminate that investment.

What most traders could not understand, how could a market go down for ten years? Human frailty rears its ugly head and says it must go up, so they kept investing. This is called averaging down. They should have been standing on the sidelines looking and waiting. They made their living from the market in years gone by. That was no longer available to them. Their living expenses were high and they never realized, until it was too late, that the game was over.

Jesse's problem, when he invested long, was the market went sideways or advanced in small increments and he made no money. When he invested short, the market went sideways, or if it did go in the direction he expected, it was not enough to cover his exorbitant expenses and the debits continued to pile up. Jesse's mental health kept deteriorating, coupled to the pressure of staving off bankruptcy once again. Add to that his much older age, the many lawsuits he was facing, and the pain that his life held.

Those of you who have experienced depression know the anguish of it. Life no longer held a fascination for him, and he could not carry on. As he wrote in his suicide note, it was incumbent upon him to end it.

Consider this: there are many excuses for failure, but none for success.

The securities market is an art, not a science.

Cornerstones
  Persistence
  Tenacity

William Crapo Durant
Originator of General Motors

Born December, 1861

The man the world forgot, the giant who almost single-handedly brought our country and the world into the Automobile Age, the Architect of wondrous things that are a part of our everyday life, I have nothing but the most profound veneration for William "Billy" Durant.

An incident that occurred early in his career was particularly fortuitous. As young William was hurrying to a meeting of the local utility company where he was an officer, he stopped and carried on a conversation with Josiah Dort, who was part owner of the hardware store. One of the employees of the hardware store, Johnny

Alger, pleasantly asked Durant if he would like a ride to the meeting in his new acquisition, a cart with a new type of suspension system. Billy, who was usually in a hurry, agreed to the offer.

As Billy rode to his meeting in this horse cart that looked like it belonged as a sulky in a trotting race, he gradually became aware of how pleasurable that this ride was. It had an absence of the inexorable bumping and swaying side to side that other carts of its day were imbued with. He immediately charged over to the factory where this cart was produced, The Cold Water Road Cart Co., and introduced himself to a little older man that he took to be the owner.

The old fellow had little to say and wondered what this audacious individual wanted. Billy, being familiar with craftsmen who had little to say, and preferred to let their hands do the talking, started by asking if he was the owner of that fine establishment that made this well-built cart. Finally, the old fellow introduced himself, not without some trepidation.

"I am Thomas O'Brian. What is the nature of your visit?"

Billy then extolled the virtues of the little cart that O'Brian had put together. Being the businessman that he was, he carefully pointed out the superior characteristics, but at the same time, held his enthusiasm back a little. He then went on to say that he was an experienced salesman and thought he could increase the sales of this vehicle if he could purchase a portion of the business. Thomas looked him in the eye trying to ascertain the seriousness of his offer. After a length of time, having not spoken a word, he turned around, walked into the next room, and eventually returned with another gentleman in tow. He introduced this person as his partner. William H. Schmedlen.

"It is my understanding that you wish to purchase this business," Schmedlen said. Billy, a little embarrassed, hurriedly went on to explain he only meant a portion of the entity, being that he did not have much in the way of funds at this time.

"We're not interested in partners," Schmedlen said. "Too many hands in the soup would spoil the broth. However, if you could produce $1500 dollars, we may be persuaded to sell lock, stock, and barrel."

Billy was surprised at the small amount of money it would take to acquire this delightful and handsome cart. Not having the $1,500 in hand, his keen mind started working on where these funds might be obtained.

Billy's middle name Crapo carried an immense amount of weight in the state; the name was prominent because his grandfather Henry Crapo had been the governor of Michigan and many of his relatives worked in the financial industry. Billy had no intention of asking them for the money, thinking, if he failed in this under taking, it would reflect badly on his entrepreneurial skills and diminish his reputation among the very people that he might approach for funding in the future. This is not to say that Billy did not approach this new exciting opportunity with the complete confidence and enthusiasm he would use to approach every business deal in the future. Durant did not know it at the time, but his future was probably going to be transcendent with this one transaction.

Billy eventually contacted a bank that was willing to loan him the money. A gentleman by the name of Robert J. Whaley was the loan officer and Durant, in later years, would credit this man with the establishment of General Motors and reward him handsomely.

In 1901, Durant was growing bored with the carriage business, which was going along nicely and did not need his attention. He found a rather new interest: the stock market. This appealed to Billy's natural instincts. Gambling and action was what he craved, not only that, the market was in its ascendancy and quite a bit of money was being made there.

Being the optimistic sort, Billy scored large gains that seemed to him to be manna from heaven, but it was only because of his expertise in business, and his ability to size up a company that he felt able to divine its future, or so he thought. When a market break came along, he always thought it would eventually return to its winning ways, and in those days, he was right. However, when the 1930s came along the market continued down year after dreary year and 1929, before the crash, would be the zenith of Billy's meteoric career.

Unhappily married, Durant stayed away from home as much as he could and the stock market was his excuse to stay in New York, where Wall Street was located, and return home infrequently. His wife, Clara, and their two children, Margery and Russell, were left behind in Flint, Michigan. Because Billy had an inherent regard for principles that had guided his life, he spent much of his time while away from home in a deep funk, since his belief system was one that would not allow him to spend time with other women.

During this period of his life, he had tried to resign from the board of his own company, but the other directors would not hear of it. This move by the other officers would lead to his eventual return to Flint and a progression into the flourishing automobile business.

Remember that much success is brought about by falling into a stinky hole and arising clean and refreshed. I believe that every person experience's this progression many times in their life. It will happen when you least expect it. Just remember you must recognize it when these things happen. Usually it is at first identified as something that is unfortunate. Later you come to the realization that you have been handed a gift that you can change from a Sows ear into a silk purse.

This happened to Billy many times in his life. On one occasion it became a defining moment; an officer in his company due to hard work was experiencing great fatigue and mental anxiety. Billy thought it would be a good idea to send him and his wife on an extended vacation on the continent.

A trusted lieutenant, A. B. Hardy, was near to collapse. Billy could see this happening and suggested Hardy take his wife on an extended European excursion. This turned out to be an excursion that would change the entire world for him and for Billy.

While in Paris, Hardy attended the Paris Exposition, which was thoroughly enjoyable and piqued his interest in a newfangled gadget that had been around for a few years, but seemed certain to become more popular.

Horseless Carriage

At first, Hardy could not see why. They were called horseless carriages and were essentially a cart with a small, one-cylinder motor that was noisy, weak, emitting smokey foul-smelling fumes that were unpleasant to the senses, but had one redeeming feature: it could get from point A to point B without the use of a horse. Hardy studied this new thing with growing interest, and finally, excitement set in. His communications to Durant showed his attraction for this faddish device and thought there was a possibility this motor driven vehicle could be improved upon for commercial gain.

Billy, surprisingly, was unimpressed. He was already aware of this new invention and thought of all the drawbacks it had, among them nauseating fumes and smoke that emanated from this contraption and don't even mention, frightening horses. It was one time in his life that his vision was not intact. Of course, it's hard to understand why his zeal was less than what one would expect from a visionary, but Billy had compelling reasons that clouded his vision. We must realize that he was the grand master in the U. S. A. of carriages. If this new fad caught on, it certainly would threaten the cornerstone of his wealth. Of course he went on to establish the greatest motor corporation in the world.

Unfortunately due to gambling instincts that was endemic to Billy's nature he was eventually deposed as the CEO of General Motors. This event occurred because of Billy's penchant of using General Motors stock as collateral to buy a host of other companies that eventually did nothing to help, placing GM in a precarious position.

This shocked Billy but it did nothing to alter his ego or ambitions. Using God given talents he embarked on a crusade to reacquire what he felt his rightful position as President of GM.

It wasn't long before he met and charmed a racecar driver by the name of Louis Chevrolet who had ambitions of building a beautiful luxury auto. Billy wasted no time in putting this idealized individual to work in his own factory, and so the Chevrolet Corporation came to be.

Chevrolet became large enough to acquire GM. And Billy again became President of the world's largest automobile manufacturing company.

It wasn't long before his old ways returned; Involved in the same thing, putting GM in debt, the bankers again decided to eliminate Billy.

So once more he found himself on the outside looking in, but his natural inclination was to gravitate to speculation in the stock market which satisfied his nature, personality, temperament, and disposition.

Unbelievably he entered the market at a time that it began a run almost unequaled in history at that time. Give the devil his due; Billy made many millions of dollars up until 1929. Now it's not what you are thinking. He did not lose it all in the 1929 crash. Actually he wisely liquidated most of his assets at the very beginning of 1929 when the market had reached an all-time high thus he escaped the slaughter that occurred at the end of October. When the bell rang it was the end of the greatest bull market we had ever seen and the beginning of a dive into agony, misery, and suffering; in other words a nightmare.

The old cry "The Market will return" made it heard. The same old dogma that we hear today. But it is not without some merit. In the roaring twenties stocks did turn around after a Sharp decline and in a short time characteristically went higher, but no more, the devastating thirty's were here and here to stay for quite a while.

Billy absolutely loved the action in the market and it was not in his nature to remain on the sidelines, consequently he tried to do what had always worked for him in the past.

The game was over, everything he tried to do no longer worked. The magic was gone and eventually so was his money.

He at one point turned to his wife, who in the past had set aside 350,000 shares of General Motors stock. These were shares Billy had given her in the eventuality that if something would happen to him, she would never be without adequate funds. Gladly she relinquished all of the stock to Billy believing in a matter of time it would be returned. He believed the country would right itself and things return to normal. It was just a matter of time before the world would be his again. Alas! It took forty years for the market to return to its height in 1929 counting for inflation.

In March 1947, Mr. William Crapo Durant passed away. He went, as we all must, in his case without a blazing epitaph, without a grand gesture, or an utterance of some declaration that we all could hold close to our hearts to be inspired by, and to have and hold for the rest of our lives. There was none of that. The man who gave us an age that changed, not only the way we lived, but also the very landscape of our country with bridges, and highways that go from coast to coast, to every hamlet in the country ... Simply, quietly, expired.

The future

Cornerstones
    Motivation
    Enthusiasm
    Equals
    Salesmanship

Bernard Baruch
Economist to Seven Presidents
Born August 19, 1870
Camden, South Carolina

Bernard was an ordinary boy who became an extraordinary man.

Handsome and tall with an imposing stature, a voice that could be strong or soft and placating without being submissive, but very much a man of considered opinions. He was a graduate of City College of New York. Even though his education was seemingly ordinary he made up for it by his foresight and intellectual gifts.

Those gifts came to fruition when Bernie was appointed chairman of the War Industries Board during the First World War under President Woodrow Wilson and remained in that position through the completion of the Second World War under President Franklin Roosevelt and as he neared doddering elder age during the Korean Police action he acted in concert with President Eisenhower to bring some semblance of order to a recalcitrant dictator of North Korea.

During the New Deal years he was a member of Roosevelt's Brain Trust His closeness to Roosevelt was demonstrated when the both of them turned a two-week vacation getaway into one month at Bernard's beautiful Hobcaw plantation in South Carolina.

It's worth quoting words from his own book published in 1957 when he had attained the age of 87:

"As a boy I was shy and fearful, with a dread of speaking in public. I had an ungovernable temper. As I grew older I liked to gamble, - A horse race, ball game, or prizefight still thrill me and make me feel young again."

"Let me interject, what he had to say was a description of many of us. It was certainly an uncanny portrayal of the successful men and women I had known in the past." Bernard goes on to say:

"Whatever I saw others accomplish, I was driven to try to do myself. Only after much effort did I learn how to control my feelings and what I could do best leaving what I could not do well to others."

"My years in Wall Street and business, in fact, became one long course of education in human nature, nearly always the problem that arose in the Stock Exchange or in other business dealings was how to disentangle the impersonal facts of a situation from the elements of human psychology which came with these facts. When I left Wall Street to go into public life I found myself confronted with this same eternal riddle-how to balance the nature of things in this world in which we live with the nature of mankind."

Aggressive moves by those we referred to as Robber Barons

In the early eighteen and nineteen hundreds money was made buying and controlling companies through the use of stock or options on stock or commitments through friends or business contacts that may be indebted to you in some manner. Using this type of pressure would put an antagonist in a position to profit handsomely by making the board of directors accede to his demands.

This could take the form of representation in an arrangement of being awarded a seat or seats on the board of directors or having the company buy the aggressors stock and options at a higher price you and your accomplice's control. Be aware that other considerations may be in the works that may have nothing to do with the current situation but involve another entity entirely and would be beneficial to the original predators.

Assume for a moment that your syndicate owns a company that makes a product that is currently being used by the object company. Your control or threat of control could be a factor in your company or companies selling more products.

Other ways of gaining influence to enhance financial futures was practiced diligently. Keep your eyes and ears wide open and make contacts with influential people. Bernie would never accept a statement from anybody unless he could establish it as a fact, no matter the prominence that person enjoyed. He learned this lesson the hard way.

As a young struggling stockbroker he overheard a conversation between two people one of which was a gentleman who had a reputation of being astute in the selection of securities. The gentleman after being asked if he knew anything about a particular security quietly related to the interested party that he thought the stock would do well in the future. Upon overhearing the conversation Bernie immediately made his way to the nearest post and invested much of his remaining assets in acquiring this stock that he was sure would make him a fortune. Of course the exact opposite happened, Bernard lost just about everything he had saved up to that point.

When he confronted the Gentleman about this occurrence, the Gentleman was rather taken-aback by this foolish person standing in front of him. He gave Bernie a puzzled look, one that said what kind of a fool are you and loudly told Bernie that he was not speaking to Bernie when he gave that information and certainly was not intended for him.

The difference between Bernard and others he had intercourse with, was the amount of time it took to absorb what life was trying to teach them. Not only life but also an improbable past is an intrusion that you learn from, and then get past it as soon as you can. Do not let it be an impediment to a bright future.

No matter what despicable, dastardly or shameful thing you have to deal with, do you honestly believe this hasn't happened in the past, millions of times? So if you think what is currently causing you an undue amount of anguish is not easily solved, think again, you would be wrong, it has been solved millions of times in the past.

If I may revisit yesteryear you will find the same thing that we are facing in our present administration. As I write this, it was acted out almost verbatim in 1935 eighty-two years ago. The following appeared in Wikipedia:

"The Nye Committee, officially known as the Special Committee on Investigation of the Munitions Industry, was a United States Senate committee (April 12, 1934– February 24, 1936), chaired by U.S. Senator Gerald Nye (a Republican). The committee investigated the financial and banking interests that underlay the United States' involvement in World War I, and was a significant factor in public and political support for American neutrality in the early stages of World War II."

"During the 1920s and 1930s, dozens of books and articles appeared which argued that arms manufacturers had tricked the United States into entering World War I. One of the best-known and deeply informed critics was Smedley D. Butler, a Major General in the U.S. Marine Corps, who published the book "War is a Racket in 1935.""

Bernard Baruch under intense investigation - War profiteering

"The Nye Committee conducted 93 hearings and questioned more than 200 witnesses. One of the persons under fire was Bernie for profiting from his position during the war because of his standing in the government. The first hearings were in September 1934 and the final hearings in February 1936. The hearings covered four topics:

The munitions industry - Bidding on Government contracts in the shipbuilding industry

War profits - The background leading up to U.S. entry into World War I.

"Although the committee found scant hard evidence to support the widespread public belief that the profits of the arms industry had been a significant factor in America's decision to participate in the war, their reports did little to dispel the notion. The committee documented the huge profits that arms factories had made during the war. It found that bankers had pressured Wilson to intervene in the war in order to protect their loans abroad. Also, the arms industry was at fault for price fixing and held excessive influence on American foreign policy leading up to and during World War I."

According to the United States Senate website: "The investigation came to an abrupt end early in 1936. The Senate cut off committee funding after Chairman Nye blundered into an attack on the late Democratic President Woodrow Wilson. Nye suggested that Wilson had withheld essential information from Congress as it considered a declaration of war.

Democratic leaders, including Appropriations Committee Chairman Carter Glass of Virginia, unleashed a furious response against Nye for 'dirt daubing the sepulcher of Woodrow Wilson.' Standing before cheering colleagues in a packed Senate Chamber, Glass slammed his fist onto his desk until blood dripped from his knuckles."

It is interesting to note on this committee was a man later accused of being a spy for the Russian Government.

Alger Hiss was convicted of perjury and served several years in a federal penitentiary.

The Baruch's gift to the USA
Hobcaw Barony

Between 1905 and 1907, Bernard Baruch systematically purchased a total of approximately 16,000 acres (63 square kilometers) of the former 18th century Hobcaw Barony, consolidating 14 plantations located on a peninsula called Waccamaw Neck between the Winyah Bay and the Atlantic Ocean, in Georgetown County, South Carolina. Baruch subsequently developed sections of the property as a winter hunting resort. He later sold the property to his eldest child, Belle W. Baruch. Upon her death in 1964, the property was transferred to The Belle W. Baruch Foundation as the Hobcaw Barony educational and research preserve.

The property also includes 37 historic buildings representing the 18th and 19th century rice cultivation industry, and early-to-mid 20th century winter resorts. The entire property was named to the National Register of Historic Places on November 2, 1994. It is administered by two South Carolina Colleges; South Carolina University and Clemson University who just happen to be bitter instate rivals as far as their sports programs were concerned. This is a man that devoted most of his life to not only the USA. But to his fellow man.

He once said that Millions of people have seen an apple fall, only Isaac Newton asked why.

He was the epitome of a speculator and made untold fortunes in the stock market.

His mantra; A speculator is a man who observes the future, and acts before it occurs.

Cornerstones
- Action
- Conviction
- Conservativism
- Philanthropy

Richard Whitney

President of the New York Stock Exchange
**Convicted Embezzler
Being led away after his trial**

Gertrude Sands Whitney

Convicted of embezzlement

Richard Whitney sitting at his desk at 23 Wall Street in the middle of the financial capital of the world reached for his handkerchief, fumbling it momentarily as he wiped a small amount of perspiration from his forehead. A monetary explosion on the morning of October 24, 1929 drew the most noted financial experts of the day to a Wall Street hastily called meeting.

The stock market was in free fall losing 11 percent of its value after the opening bell. The actual loss was probably much steeper, the ticker tape was running several hours behind, and the carnage from margin and panic selling was unknown. The bankers took immediate action and decided to invest millions of dollars into the bloodbath. This day would change Richard's life forever.

The bankers and the essential investors attending that meeting had decided Richard Whitney was the man that carried enough significance to instill confidence in the brokers crowding around the various posts.

Richard, fastidious as always, stood up and assumed the posture of a confident man. Over six feet tall his total image gave the impression of loftiness. He strode to the trading floor with an impervious air, as if nothing to be concerned about, his attitude seemed to be; I'll take care of this matter as quickly as possible and then get on with the days business.

Richard was anything but calm, at that moment he had many emotions churning inside. Yes, he was losing money and that caused some consternation. Yet his greater emotion, the thing that really drove Richard Whitney was his quest for recognition from his peers.

On this day he appeared to reach the pinnacle of his profession. However he had not a clue what was just days away. He absolutely believed that he and the bankers would avert any decline in the stock market as they had in the past and things would again return to normal and the market continue its ascent as it had for most of the 20's.

Thus began the odyssey of the most horrendous crash the stock market had ever experienced.

Born into a heritage that fostered success and a well-respected family, Richard, seemingly on a great career path, eventually succumbed to a path less traveled by his family. His thirst for prominence in his own right overtook his good sense.

Can you believe that history repeated once again the follies of abundance and for the second time to the former head of the New York Stock Exchange? The charge was embezzlement. If you don't believe that, let me give you one name that will change your thinking. "Bernard Madoff" Absolutely the greatest swindler of all time. Yes, and both of them had risen to a position of prodigious power with proven personal abilities, not the least being abundant intelligence.

What was the flaw in their character that would cause them to do immense harm to other people?

Whitney's great imperfection; wanting to live in an extravagant manner his income could not support. He had an inherent disregard for other people beautifully hidden behind his fallacious façade of respectability. Consequently his ability to acquire funds from friends, family, and clients was largely unimpeded.

His modus of operation;

To exude an aura of great respectability, so as to imbue confidence from his peers. This is not a character flaw unless carried to its extreme.

To give the impression of bountiful financial success which garners recognition from your contemporaries?

The image of an intelligent gambler being fearless and able to plunge prudently with a demeanor of haughty responsibility to your colleagues.

There was so much respect he commanded, that whenever crises occurred Richard would be the pick of other financial savants to lead the charge to bring financial markets back to equilibrium. To be able to do this was to bring men of wealth together, pooling their assets and injecting fresh funds and biding high profile stocks into higher ground thereby turning around the insidious decline of stocks and giving confidence to investors. It was a tactic that had a history of success.

In 1929 the man picked for this important mission was none other than Richard Whitney.

Whitney became a member of a number of the city's elite social clubs and was appointed treasurer of the New York Yacht Club. In 1919, he was elected to the Board of Governors of the New York Stock Exchange and not long thereafter was named its vice-president.

PANIC

On October 24, 1929, Black Thursday, he attempted to avert the Wall Street Crash of 1929.

Alarmed by rapidly falling stock prices, several leading Wall Street bankers met to find a solution to the panic and chaos on the trading floor of the New York Stock Exchange. The meeting included Thomas W. Lamont, acting head of Morgan Bank; Albert Wiggin, head of the Chase National Bank; and Charles E. Mitchell, president of the National City Bank of New York and other high profile financers. They chose Whitney, then vice president of the Exchange, to act on their behalf.

With the bankers' financial resources behind him, Whitney went onto the floor of the Exchange and went directly to the post of U.S. Steel and under the intense watch of the other traders flamboyantly placed a bid to purchase a large block of shares in U.S. Steel at a crazy price well above the current market.

As traders watched, Whitney then placed similar bids on other "blue chip" stocks. This tactic was analogous to a tactic that had ended the Panic of 1907, and succeeded in halting the slide that day. The Dow Jones Industrial Average recovered with a slight decrease, closing down only 6.38 points for that day. In this case, however, the respite was only temporary; stocks subsequently collapsed catastrophically on Black Tuesday, October 29. Whitney's actions gained him the sobriquet, "White Knight of Wall Street."

Ron Chicone

This event did much to enhance Whitney's reputation, but what happened you may ask, to the brace of bankers and other men of massive amounts of money. They held a meeting the morning of that faithful day and did what they always did in times of crises, if their first foray did not do the job they expected; the next thing on the agenda was to preserve their wealth.

The rich were not always the bastions of public service.

The mantra; if you are bigger than the situation; stand your ground and fight; if the adversary was the equal of you, than use your power of oral persuasion; if however the opposition gave indications that this operation may be costly, use your third option; turn and run for the nearest exits and find a way to make more money. Their experience had taught them to never hang on to a losing position. When their effort to come to the rescue of the millions of little people didn't work; then find a way to make money even if it hurt the vast majority of investor's. They sold the market "short."

It is a method that the majority of investors are not familiar. In a nutshell it means to borrow stock you do not own and sell it now while the market is declining than buy it back and replace it when you feel the market has bottomed.

The investor profits by the difference between what he originally sold it, which would have been at a higher price and buy it back at a lower price and replace the borrowed shares. That method exacerbates the markets decline hurting the many small investors and in many instances wiping away what little they have left.

Yes, that seems cruel, but the lesson you must learn; you are not investing to lose money. That being said, the lesson is, never think that the other person has a heart of gold and wants nothing more than for you to succeed.

Eventually Richard because of his unsullied reputation up to that time was appointed President of the New York Stock Exchange. In this capacity, he became the leading opponent of federal regulations of the securities industry, testifying in Washington, speaking around the country, but he was dealing with an indomitable force, the resolute and incomparable President Franklin Delano Roosevelt, who passed many pieces of legislation concerning financial matters, not the least being the 1933 Securities Act and the Securities Exchange Act of 1934 creating the Securities and Exchange Commission as the regulatory agency for the industry. Of course Richard opposed any legislation that would diminish the influence of the New York Stock Exchange.

Imagine if you can an investor that became the ultimate insider and went on to lose millions of dollars trading in stocks despite a lifetime of high education and experience with enormous influence and friends that defied the epithet of loser.

Richard had a penchant for the hi-life and living as if there was no end to his wealth-spring of unlimited funds, and so he did what other people did when they wanted to live beyond their means; Borrow money from one and all and when that was exhausted than steal money, or as he termed it, borrowing from wherever money was available.

In Richards's case, because of his seemingly high position in life, it became axiomatic that a great deal of trust was placed in his hands. Case in point; he was elected treasurer of his exclusive yacht club and had access to the clubs resources. Of course there was a diminishing of those assets under his administration.

Richard eventually retired as President of the New York Exchange in 1935 but retained a seat on the board of governors.

Finally the stage was set for the final indignity and a ludicrous story being told. Unbelievable to say the least.

The comptroller of the New York Exchange at last blew the whistle and established absolute proof that Richard Whitney was an embezzler and that his company was insolvent. Within a few days, the appalling news was disseminated and Whitney and his company would both declare bankruptcy. An astonished public learned of his misdeeds on March 10, 1938 when he was officially charged with embezzlement by New York County District Attorney Thomas E. Dewey.

Indicted by a grand jury, Richard Whitney was arrested pleaded guilty, and sentenced to a term of five to ten years in Sing Sing prison. On April 12, 1938, in his odyssey Richard sponged money 111 times and ended up owing many millions of dollars. His brother an executive with the Morgan interests made restitution of the entire amount that Richard had embezzled.

This act in and of itself showed what the Whitney's were made of. One black sheep did not make the whole.

During the entire time of the court proceedings, Richard refused to lower his head. Dogmatically he marched into the court as if his entrance was that of a King's coronation rather than the subjugation of a thief. Unfortunately he was a thief, a thief of the worst kind; he stole from a vast array of the public not showing a bit of remorse, guilt, or repentance.

Richard became a model prisoner served a prison sentence of three years and four months. He lived quietly thereafter and died on a farm at the age of 88.

His family was by his side throughout this time in his life, showing with much personal hurt and embarrassment that they were truly a family.

Yea, verily I say, beware of the Richard Whitney's out there for there are others who believe in their nobility and will have their hand in your pocket, though they would be appalled if someone referred to them as a crook.

Cornerstones

Let history be your instructor.

James Buchanan Brady

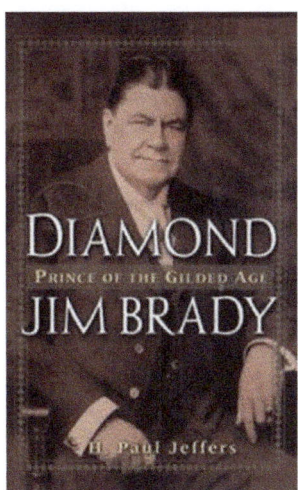

Diamond Jim Brady
August 12, 1856

In our lives we always have time for the Characters, diverse and unique among us. One such person has gone down in history in such a way that historical antiquity will never forget him. His persona is indescribable, he was so far away from the norm in his manner of dress, his swagger, his bigger than life appearance, at 6'2" three hundred and plus pounds with a personality that was glittering and on fire, precious gems were elegantly festooned about his body, while he escorted attractive women to the various dance halls where he was an accomplished dancer. No one could ever forget him.

Dan Brady's Saloon was the cocoon that nourished Jim Brady. Coming from a family that was tough, hard drinking Irishmen did not seem the most likely place for a future legend of the American scene to be raised, but it worked for Jim. He absolutely idolized his father, so what he learned at an early age were many things that the average schoolboy never has a chance to observe. The first thing it taught was abstinence from the debilitating effects of the demon Rum. The second thing was maybe the most important, the ability to win a fight without fighting. We're talking about personality here folks. The kind of personality that enabled Jim to become one of the richest men of the Gilded Age.

He has been described variously as kind, ostentatious, a galvanizing salesman, a vast overeater that was legendary, but the overeating obsession was enormously embellished.

However Food was one of his passions and enjoyment in life contributing to his unappetizing obese appearance.

To bring his character together requires quite a stretch. Not only was he flamboyant in everything he did but he could back it up with many millions of dollars accumulated with intelligent investments in the stock market and mainly commissions selling railroad equipment plus other ventures that were speculative in nature to say the least. Although moral in most aspects he was not above constructing a supposition in such a way, whether legal or illegal, making himself the beneficiary of the proceeds.

As a young man he had a vision of where his future would be. To attain that lofty level required much study and work. Every step along the way became a new challenge with more knowledge and expertise required, but more than that was his ability to charm and make a friend out of everyone he met whether a street cleaner or the head of a great company. It mattered not to Jim; he had this innate ability to be interested in each person he encountered.

So it came about; all of his acquaintances became instant close comrades and whenever Jim needed confirmation he would be surrounded with close friends; and that is the hallmark of a super salesman.

Diamond Jim came along when the railroads were just coming of age. The trans-continental road came into existence and the rails were joined at a place called Promontory Summit, Utah May 10, 1869

This event foretold the great migration to the west which would become the precursor to the greatest nation in the world. During Jim's time he followed the money and the railroads was the place to invest and with foresight and instant recognition Jim attached his wagon to this burgeoning enterprise. He became a salesman of railroad equipment.

Lillian Russell

His natural affinity for getting close to people served him well in this profession. One of his great friends was the leading lady of the day, Lillian Russell. I believe this was a strong committed friendship and it may have been more, but each kept their feelings private. He was seen with a great many of the famous beauties of the day. A ready dancer and noted partier, Jim loved to be seen with a famous beauty on his arm. His love for diamonds extended to these lovelies. They loved diamonds too and Jim was only too happy to supply them with the newest fashion jewelry of the season.

Railroads were the King, Queen, and principal Consort of America during the 1800's all the way to 1930, when the advent of interstates along with declining revenue from passenger service brought a pause in the earnings of railroads.

If you were a buyer for a railroad and you needed anything from a wrench to a cowcatcher, the person you went to see was Diamond Jim Brady. The buyer more than likely counted Jim as a friend; of course he wanted to do business with a friend. Jim's super salesmanship was legendary. He was so wealthy from earned commissions it was once told he bet one million dollars on the turn of a card and won.

Jim's showmanship was incomparable. His office was Broadway. It was a great privilege to be entertained by this extraordinary man. Most all buyers could not wait for an invitation to be sold some item by the great man himself.

What made Jim so desirable to potential buyers?

Each person was made to feel important.

Each person became a personal friend.

Buying from Jim was an event not easily forgotten.

His office was a table in a famed restaurant.

It was a given that you would be introduced to other attendees who may be of help to your career.

Rubbing shoulders with actors and performers that were of some note certainly could be a thrill and they too were excited to be invited to Jim's table.

Jim's extravagances were mythical and that included sharing the beautiful showgirls he kept company. Surprisingly they were not the main course. They came after a dinner as sumptuously appointed as any served in the great Halls of European nobility.

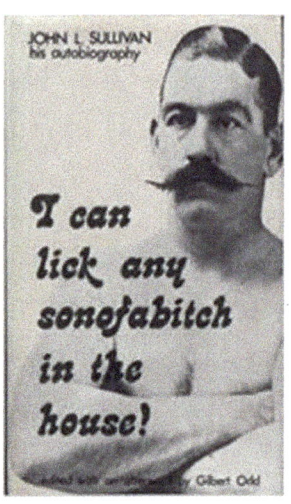 

Jim was not without his moments of derring-do. On one fortuitous evening he happened to be introduced to the bare knuckle Heavyweight Champion of the world "John L. Sullivan." In his customary manner John L. proclaimed that he could beat any sonofabitch in the bar with either his fists or drinking whiskey. Jim hearing this proposed to John L. that they sit and contemplate the merits of the finest whiskey in the house and Jim would shoulder the entire weight of the expense.

Mr. Sullivan was never known to shun the offer of a free drink, readily agreed to the proposition and so the contest was on.

Unknown to John L. the bartender a close friend of Jim's knew that Jim did not drink, so nary a drop of whiskey touched Jim's lips. An alcohol free secret substitution was employed.

After many hours of drinking John L. Sullivan barely able to hold on to the edge of the bar, decided to throw in the towel and hollered out to one and all that Diamond Jim was the goddamnest toughest man he had ever met and could not understand why in heaven's name he was still standing.

**He had an affinity for horseracing
And strong gambling instincts**

STEEL RAILROAD CARS

As perchance would have it Jim was afforded the opportunity to invest in a new technology. Railroad long haul cars were primarily constructed of durable wood in the long-ago past. In this era technology was advancing at a pace that was a little disconcerting. It was hard to figure out what was doable and what was not.

Even though steel cars were vastly superior to wood cars, cost was a big factor. Jim could produce something that was superior in every way but if the Railroad's did not find them profitable, than it was just spitting in the wind. Jim decided to take a chance. Steel cars were vastly higher in cost but the amount of freight they could carry over long distances was enormous plus their life span was greater than wood. The problem that Jim encountered was proving it.

Jim bought a steel company and produced prototypes that he could bring to companies and they could then see themselves what the benefits were.

Of course problems were a part of the business. Jim found after the fact that there were more competitors he did not know about. Now the real genius of Jim would become obvious. One by one he rounded up the various opponents and through superb salesmanship formed a trust over a two year period that included all but him, although he incorporated two friends on the board and held a large position in the stock of the company, and lo and behold who became the one and only salesmen of the firm collecting a hefty commission on each car sold? Jim of course.

The amount that Jim made from this enterprise we never knew, but it must have been untold millions. It brings to mind the old adage "where there's a will there's a way." There is never a dead end. If it appears that way, than you aren't relentless enough. Remember the answer is today, tomorrow hasn't come yet.

Jim enjoyed much success with many of the ladies on Broadway, but the one that captured his heart was a girl by the name of Edna McCauley who was an $8 a week sales girl at a department store. She was lucky enough to be introduced to Jim while he was dining at the Waldorf. Using her best availability manner she was invited to his place that evening. Whatever transpired that evening was enough to endear her to Jim for the next ten years.

During this time Jim fell deeply in love. They did discuss marriage but it never happened. Finally the end came when Jim introduced her to one of his gambling friends. They fell in love and Jim was shunted aside and suffered a considerable amount of time in a deep funk over this loss. Not to mention the amount of offerings of the world that Jim bestowed upon her inconsiderate soul.

His loss was not done in a vacuum. Surprisingly the gentleman in question, "Jessie Lewisohn" was being considered by the great Lillian Russell as her next partner in marriage. She felt a great deal of hurt when he announced that a marriage to Miss McCauley was imminent.

This event was probably lucky for both of them. The fidelity of Jessie and Edna was questionable and if not now, than sometime in the future this same scenario would take place.

Because of Jim's lifestyle he suffered a great many malady's. Being considerably overweight brought on many of his health problems.

When the physicians informed Jim of his eminent demise and recommended he spend the remainder of his life in the hospital. Jim rebelled and informed them that he would not die in a hospital. Whereupon he went to his favorite resort on the boardwalk at $1000 a week and passed away in his favorite pajama's in April 1917.

Of being Diamond Jim, he of immeasurable salesmanship abilities sold to the Government a great amount of World War 1 equipment prior to his expiration.

As Yogi Berra the Hall of Fame baseball catcher said, "it's not over till it's over."

Cornerstones

    You can never overdress. Dress for success
    Do something memorable
    Be a non-conformist
    Everybody is a friend
    Think highly of yourself
    Become the person you believe you can be
    Remember the most important thing you have to sell is "yourself"
    Self-image
    Self-worth
    Self-evaluation
    Prudent
    Let history be your instructor
    Moral personal relationships
    Persistence and Tenacity
    PROCRASTINATION, THE ULTIMATE KILLER OF DREAMS.

YOU CAN NEVER OVERDRESS. DRESS FOR SUCCESS

When the morning begins is when the selling begins. The first steps out of your house should find you resplendent. You should be at your most appealing and fetching best.

Does that sound old fashion? Well yes it is. The old truths are never out of fashion.

DO SOMETHING MEMORABLE

Okay today will be the day when you change the world. That seems like a tall order, but yes, one person can change the world. Billy Durant did it when he started General Motors. So did Edison when he lit the night.

"Wait, I know, let's start a peace movement. Let's start in one city." "Okay! Let's start in Mexico, don't they have the butterfly capital of the world." Where the Monach Butterfly's gather in the winter.

Yes, I know this seems crazy. But that's the point. Think about things that are in another dimension and then go ahead and give **YOUR BRAIN A CHANCE TO GROW.**

BE A NON-CONFORMIST

You can start by thinking of a new way and better way to do some element you do every day of your life. A new way to shave or a better way to have sex. Oh! I know you think I'm stretching it, but what the hell why not?

Do you get the idea?

EVERYBODY IS A FRIEND

The best way to have a friend is be a friend. To make a friend, stop talking and listen. Find out if there is a way to make his/her existence more exciting, more interesting, better in some manner. When you leave that person, feel that in some way you have made their life better off for having known you.

THINK HIGHLY OF YOURSELF

You really are important. You are the most important person in the world. If you were running for an elective office, would you try to hide the things that make you great, of course not? Trumpet your better qualities and let people in on the fact that you are somebody to be reckoned with.

BECOME THE PERSON YOU BELIEVE YOU CAN BE

Who do you imagine yourself to be? How close can you get to emulation of who you would like to be in your imagination?

Imagination is an outstanding part of the human condition. Anything can happen. You can fly as close to the sun as you want or take a trip to the bowels of the earth.

In your imagination, you can go and do anything you want. All you have to do is dream it and it's yours.

The most powerful thing on earth, "Your Imagination.

Let your Imagination run wild.

The houses below were built by Architect Michael Jantzen

This is what I'm talkin about. Imagination!

REMEMBER THE MOST IMPORTANT THING YOU HAVE TO SELL IS "YOURSELF"

I'm the person you been waiting to meet. I know you did not know that, but this is your lucky day because you are going to meet me, and from now on, your life will be better.

This is what you should feel from the top of your head to the tip of your toes. Now, guess what? You will absolutely find a way to make that person better today than he or she was yesterday.

Happiness is contagious and you are the vendor.

SELF-IMAGE

You are who you think you are feelings can make you successful

In every creature there is something that makes them beautiful.

Have you seen a turtle? He has to be certainly one of the ugliest creatures alive.

Take a closer second look. Suddenly you realize he is truly a wonder of the universe, absolutely beautiful in a way that is indescribable.

Look in the mirror. Your damn right, I am good-looking.

I can see the energy overflowing.
To-day will possibly become the greatest day of my life.
Because I am who I think I am.

SELF-WORTH

What you do in life has a value to SOMEBODY; it could be your family or possibly a person that's down on their luck.

Using your success to help somebody else or a worthy CHARITABLE ORGANIZATION. That's what life is all about.

"Brother can you spare a dime."

SELF-EVALUATION

The ability to see yourself as others see you is a talent reserved for those of us who have the capacity to be self-critical. Not many have that capability. Possibly a good thing.

It is worth remembering anything can be over-done. Your aggrandizement is important to all that you do.

Become a legend in your own mind.

PRUDENT

Making life joyful and hassle free is not possible and that goes without saying. Of course no life is hassle free. Without challenges is life worth living? That would be a negative.

My own life seemed many times to have been on the edge of insanity. For me the quest for instant riches was a constant anomaly that led me to make horrible mistakes and heart-rending decisions not only for myself but also for others who got in the way of the madman that was steamrolling all before him.

My wayward pursuits finally brought me to a point that culminated in West Palm Beach, Florida.

On a bright December Florida morning as I scurried away from my citadel of the moment, a buck a night flop house where the cockroaches were so numerous they would have honestly made a good meal, I can say that, because it had been about three or four days since I had been able to afford a feast I only remembered, I started to enter my "Chariot". A recent vintage convertible that had been purchased with good intentions but alas as fortune would have it I was in arrears on the required payments demanded by the real owners of the car; The credit company.

Two gentlemen dressed in blue approached and informed me I had another area that needed attention: unpaid parking tickets. This seemed to be a matter that they took seriously and because of my lack of coin of the realm they deemed it necessary to escort me to the local confinement center commonly referred to as a jail.

I knew only one person that would help and he was out of town for the evening which meant that I would have new accommodations until the sun comes up in the morning.

You can only imagine how down in the dumps I felt that evening as I contemplated my current plight, sitting on the steel springs of a fold down chained cot.

I went from a rat-infested buck a night flophouse to the most well-built building in town in one day. You may laugh, but it was an event that contributed to my eventual success in life. It started me on the path to becoming prudent.

Without prudence, wealth you acquire is only temporary. It may come to you but keeping it will be beyond your ability to control.

Spending without purpose, realism, or regard for future goals, certainly should bring under suspicion your grasp of reality or your innate intelligence level if one exists at all.

Summing up; prudent in the order of importance in the list of Cornerstones will be in the top three.

LET HISTORY BE YOUR INSTRUCTOR

You may think of history as archaic, decrepit, hoary, and riddled with green mossy stuff and known instances of boredom found in the institutes of this nation.

You would be wrong. Just open the Book of Knowledge. It is filled with history, the only place that all wisdom has been assembled.

What's that you say? It doesn't apply to me. Wow, wrong again!

If you want to be successful in any endeavor; make a study of history. If you become proficient and immersed in the art of antiquity you will find the relevance of this book to be lessened. My attempt here is to capture the essence of investing. Every bit of wisdom disseminated here, has been cultivated from the pages of the Book of Knowledge.

"Hello! What's that you say? You're kidding, the book of knowledge? Never heard of it. Where can I find this book and who the hell wrote it?"

If you want to find that manuscript, it is easily accessible in thousands of buildings across this country.

Written by thousands and thousands of scholars, intellectuals, and knowledgeable noted issue of scions, it's called a "Library" Look in the history section.

MORAL PERSONAL RELATIONSHIPS

Morality is an old-fashioned word. We use it according to whatever relationship it has to you. It can be used to discern traits we inherently believe are part and parcel of what we believe is the way we have lived our lives.

In each one of us, resides that mendacious double-dealing organism that's going to meet the guy with the pitchfork and the cloven hooves. Not one of us alive today is without sin, so stop beating yourself up; you are part of the human race.

There is a truism; always in any transaction made between you and another person it must and will be honored. It means every aspect of an agreement be strictly adhered too, including all inferences, extrapolations, and insinuations that were never explicitly spelled out.

In business your reputation and honor means the whole endeavor may never take place if your rectitude is in question. This has an absolute bearing on success or failure.

PERSISTENCE AND TENACITY

The chain that binds the lives I have highlighted is the principal of persistence and tenacity. Without these commonality's they become not even a mention in history.

Certainly you have seen this for yourself. No matter where you have been or what position you have occupied on the ladder of success, the people that clawed their way over you had these traits.

Add in the other cornerstones plus the most important one of all "DREAMS" and you have become unbeatable.

If I may, I will reiterate:

Always follow your dreams.

They are there for a reason and that will be the foundation of all the success you will have in the future.

And now I have revealed the first secret to victory in the pursuit of money.

Nothing can hold you back except for one thing, "YOUR HEALTH" and that is up to the "prudent you" and not in the purview of this book.

PROCRASTINATION
THE ULTIMATE KILLER OF DREAMS

Have you ever looked across the room and suddenly there she is! A vision of loveliness. You notice that her gaze slowly revolves around the area and for just a moment lingers on you, my god man, opportunity exists, why are you standing there hesitating? Point YOU'RE feet in her direction and in just a few steps you can change your entire life.

I will not speculate whether the outcome will be a positive or not, but damn you will never know unless you take action and get your feet moving. In just a moment or two she is leaving and again the emptiness in your life is closing in.

The most successful investors are opportunists; swashbucklers, speculators, buccaneers, or activists with a measure of background information which can be very effective.

Many times opportunity is right before our eyes but it can be fleeting so action is required at that moment and not a second later.

Theodore Roosevelt Said;

"In any moment of decision, the best thing you can do is the right thing. The worst thing you can do is nothing." — Theodore Roosevelt

SO, GO GET EM COWBOY AND DON'T FORGET TO SMELL THE ROSES AND HAVE FUN ALONG THE WAY.

$ CHAPTER TWO $
In The Beginning

Psycho-Cybernetics and The Silva Mind Control Method

These two books by Maxwell Maltz M.D. and Jose Silva are very worthwhile reads. Dr. Maltz, a plastic surgeon, emphasizes the marvelous power and abilities each of us has inherited from the creator. Jose Silva carries the power of the mind to extreme conclusions and shows how to utilize imagination. Have you heard of creating a useful laboratory in the brain that comes complete with advisors which will show you the way to unimaginable abilities?

Yes, I have now entered the realm of disbelief. Many of you will make light of the following magic utterances, shame on you, do you really have a mind that actually closes down when faced with a new and far-out concept? Well take a step back and reconsider the many miracles that have occurred in our time on this earth: powered Flight, electricity, self-driving cars, cell phones, the internet. We can now fly across continents and oceans in literally hours that used to take weeks and months Electricity is so prolific that our life is virtually filled with wondrous devices, contraptions, and thingamajigs that put us to bed at an angle that makes restful moments heaven on earth and lets us get in a car that has the ability to drive itself. Phones give us the ability to talk to someone on the next continent, not only that, but now you can see them while talking to the phone, yes you can even talk to a "person" that's not even there. The internet gives us access to information instantly.

Here again you must use prudence and lucidity and come to a conclusion that enhances your bank account and the capacity to be a contributor to the many people and things that need a helping hand. Not to mention enhancing your livability on a higher plane.

Doctor Maltz encourages deep relaxation, Jose Silva uses a form of self-hypnosis referred to as going to levels which are Beta (awake and in the moment), Alpha (dreaming), Theta (a partial dreaming state), Delta (deep sleep).

The good Doctor Maltz encourages his patients to utilize meditation and relaxation to change their self-image. When he exposed them to meditation he could achieve amazing results. When he explored this technique further he improved their health and even their athletic ability, not just self-image.

Jose Silva takes it many steps further than Dr. Maltz. It is his contention you can improve to an unbelievable level your natural extra sensory perception (ESP). You can improve your abilities to a degree that can be classified as sensational.

To make all of this work you must be positive. Negativity will boomerang and can be detrimental.

So let's distill this information to give us the capability and expertise to bring enormous success in our quest to achieve mega amounts of money. This will only work if you realize that making money for yourself is not the goal. Making scads of wampum is to be used to help all of humanity.

If selfishness is your goal than stop reading now, this book will not help you.

There are so many things unknown to us in this universe. It's hard to put everything into its little niche and call it a truth. There are phenomena that we all have experienced; ESP is prevalent among people that have been together for a period of time.

A personal experience occurred at a time in my life when the game of golf was upper most in my existence. I had a close friend that was just as dedicated a golfer as I. At the time, we played every day and perpetually I was on the losing end of the bet. My practice schedule was extreme whereas my friend seemed to shoot outstanding games never picking up a golf club from one day to the next. Finally, I became frustrated and I asked him what his secret was. He said "Ron you wouldn't believe me if I told you," "I said okay I won't believe you, let's hear it anyway." He continued, "I know you will think I'm crazy but each night as I lie in bed, in a relaxed state of mind, I think of my golf game and review each hole I played, and then I bring to the forefront where I could improve my game and for a few moments I practice in my head what I want to change and invariably the next day I solved my problem."

I eventually adhered to this method and dramatically improved my game enough that I eventually won many amateur tournaments. This method is applicable to every problem you will have in life.

Wow, did you read and understand what I just said; **that is a cataclysmic expression**, employing an easy approach to solving life's most vexing problems.

How is this applied to improving your ability to make money in the stock market? Dr. Maltz believes "human beings always act and feel and perform in accordance with what they imagine to be true about themselves and their environment."

Psycho Cybernetics utilizes a mechanical perspective of your brain and body's activity to create a new system of thinking and behaving.

"Creative striving for a goal that is important to you as a result of your own deep-felt needs, aspirations and talents (and not symbols which the "Joneses" expect you to display) brings happiness as well as success because you will be functioning as you were meant to function. Man is by nature a goal-striving being. And because man is "built that way" he is not happy unless he is functioning as he was made to function – as a goal-striver. Thus, true success and true happiness not only go together but each enhances the other."

"Whatever your definition of happiness may be, you will experience happiness only as you experience more life. More living means among other things more accomplishment, the attainment of worthwhile goals, more love experienced and given, more health and enjoyment, more happiness for both yourself and others."

Tweetable summary
Your self-image determines your self-worth.
You Make Mistakes—Mistakes Don't Make You
Experience is Important

As a plastic surgeon, he saw example after example of patients who would have their outward appearance transformed (via plastic surgery), but wouldn't end up any happier as a result of having had their surgeries. In short: their outward appearance would change, but their internal feelings and attitudes would remain the same.

People's experiences are similar to a machine's programming. Both lead to certain outcomes, and both can be changed. As the field of psychology developed, it became clear that even in a controlled laboratory, people could use experiences "imagined vividly and in detail" to change outcomes.

"Whether we realize it or not, each of us carries with us a mental blueprint or picture of ourselves...It has been built up from our own beliefs about ourselves. But most of these beliefs about ourselves have unconsciously been formed from our past experiences, our success and failures, our humiliations, our triumphs, and the way other people have reacted to us, especially in early childhood."

Although you are not conscious of it, your self-image has developed as a result of your past experiences. You tend to believe this self-image, and live your life based on this belief of yourself. This explains how some people seem to always be successful, and others constantly fail. Their subsequent experiences will support the self-image they have of themselves.

Many people's attempts at changing their self-image are external—as witnessed by Dr. Maltz in his plastic surgery practice. Some have tried positive thinking about the future, without actually addressing their beliefs about their self-image. This is where Dr. Maltz discovered the great potential for change—in directing activity at your self-image. He discovered that true happiness and satisfaction in life comes from "an adequate and realistic self-image that you can live with."

THE SECRET

Dr. Maltz sees the subconscious as a mechanism that the mind controls. He calls this our Creative Mechanism. It will function based on the goals it is given. These goals are based on your self-image. This self-image dictates the limits of your accomplishments—what you believe you can do. The Creative Mechanism uses past memories as structure for solving current problems.

Within all of us is also a Success Mechanism. This is the structure and function designed for any "activity which is intimately tied in to [your] "living" or makes for a fuller life."

In addition to your brain's amazing capabilities, there is support to the concept that your brain can access subconscious knowledge outside of its own experiences. This access to universal knowledge answers is acquired through analysis, contemplation, and striving for.

"Science has now confirmed what philosophers, mystics, and other intuitive people have long declared: every human being has been literally "engineered for success" by his Creator.

"Every human being has access to a power greater than himself."

THE IMPORTANCE OF IMAGINATION

"For imagination sets the goal "picture" which our automatic mechanism works on. We act or fail to act, not because of "will," as is so commonly believed, but because of imagination."

Your thoughts and actions are based on what you imagine as truth. Hypnosis is an excellent example of this in action. "Your nervous system reacts appropriately to what "you" think or imagine to be true."

Numerous studies have shown that mental practice improves actual performance. The key is to practice the correct mental image of the actual action.

You've already built a self-image based on past experiences. "Now you are to use the same method to build an adequate self-image that you previously used to build an inadequate one." Use 30 minutes a day to relax, close your eyes, and imagine you are watching a movie of you. Get detailed. This is your mental practice for life. View positive interactions, opportunities, responses and dreams. Don't worry if you don't believe it—that will come. Think about how each of your senses will experience what you are imagining. Imagine positive feelings that you will experience. And remember that it may take you at least 21 days of practicing this before you notice changes. Practice will lead to new, automatic responses based on the self-image you are developing.

When you are successfully hypnotized, it is because you believe what the hypnotist is saying. In this sense, you have been hypnotized throughout your life. You believe what someone has said to you or about you, and this belief has led to certain actions. Perhaps you've been told you are dumb, ugly, or bad at math. You have accepted these statements and then felt obligated to act them out in order to 'be yourself.'

The reverse of being hypnotized into negative beliefs is also possible. People have been hypnotized and behaved far beyond what their conscious restrictions would allow them. In a sense they were dehypnotized so that they could achieve what they were truly capable of Inferiority comes when we measure ourselves against someone else's 'normal' rather than our own. We believe we should be what they are, and determine that we are unworthy... NOT true. "We have allowed ourselves to be hypnotized by the entirely erroneous idea that "I should be like so-and-so". This leads to more striving, more inferiority, and a miserable life.

The solution lies in knowing that you are uniquely you, and will never be someone else. You're not supposed to be. Your uniqueness is valuable, and only yours to have.

So how do you undo these types of negative beliefs about yourself if you're holding onto them?

In order to undo a negative belief or behavior, we need to begin by relaxing.

This leads to Dr. Maltz' second practice exercise in the book—using imagination to relax. Get comfortable, and consciously relax each muscle group in your body. Don't let this be work—just do what you can easily do. Move through mental images of relaxation.

USING RATIONAL THINKING AND RELAXATION

"Scientific experiments have shown that it is absolutely impossible to feel fear, anger, anxiety, or negative emotions of any kind while the muscles of the body are kept perfectly relaxed."

Rational thinking works for changing beliefs and behaviors. You do not have to unbury every negative unconscious thought in order to change. Focusing on a mistake or guilty feelings can make the mistake the actual goal. Instead, remember that negative experiences helped you orient towards your goals, and then can be forgotten as you practice traveling in the right direction towards your goals.

Rational thoughts must be joined by feelings and desires. Long for who you want to be, and what you want to have. Get excited about these desires. This process is exactly like worrying, except that now you are dwelling on positive, desirable things instead of negative things. As you change your goal picture and engage your positive emotions the possibilities will become more real.

Conundrums

The first lesson to be learned is one of the most difficult; the price of the stock has no bearing on the amount of money you will earn.

The second lesson to be learned is to disregard the first lesson.

Now we run into our first conundrum.

So what does this teach us; simply any statement made about stocks or the stock market can be puzzling and may not be true, except for one, stocks fluctuate in value. Sometimes moderately and sometimes severely.

Be aware of the fact that over the long term stocks increase in value. Does that mean you should always keep an investment for the long run? Absolutely not; money has a cost. Money must be utilized. If you let money just sit without earning, than it is dead and will decay and wither away.

Here again we run into the dreaded conundrum; a statement that is a puzzle and possibly not true. There have been times in the past that it is better to have money sitting on the sidelines watching and waiting than being killed in a fast declining stock market. If you could go back in time and ask the likes of Jessie Livermore or the Morgan's or Billy Durant or any of the prominent men who invested in the market in the thirties, what do you think they would say?

Changing personalities and thoughts that were taught through generations of time obtained from your family, your friends, your teachers, even the part of the country where you reached maturity.

Being youthful generally leads to stronger opinions and many times expressed in actions that can be abnormally vociferous. Aging seems to have a quieting effect on attitudes and beliefs and ideas. A good thing is it not? Not necessarily, Oops, another conundrum, the young have a strangle hold on new inventions and new ways of presenting old idea's. They are the one's rioting in the streets and many times changing governments, good or bad, not for me to judge. My intellect does not rise to that level.

My only objective is to have readers change the way they perceive an investment. Please disregard all of the hype surrounding an investment; i.e.

A new product not yet on the market, earnings will be boffo;

My brother-in-law works there and knows the head janitor;

A guy I just met who has immense success, in stocks, according to him, told me in confidence this stock will double in value in the very near future;

My hairdresser told me they are waiting in line to purchase this new product.

Sorry, all of the forgoing is pure baloney. That is not the way you generally make an investment decision. Again we run into our old friend; "conundrum."

There are times that the rumors of a revolutionary new product will force you to give more scrutiny to a stock. A very old adage cries out, buy on the rumor sell on the fact. Let's turn this old adage on its back and take a look in its more personal spots.

I want to play the "what if game." What if I happened to be one of the ten or more sitting on the board of directors of a company? One morning attending a meeting of this board with the required coffee and doughnut sitting before me, the CEO arose and established the fact that this morning's meeting was a very special get together that would determine the future of the company. "Gentleman" he announced, "we have been secretly working on plans developing a product that will revolutionize the entire core of this country." With that statement hanging in the air he brought in and introduced the engineers that had made it possible.

After a question and answer period, the good feelings that abounded in this room were overwhelming. In my briefcase sitting on the floor beside me, were the papers to be filled out on options that would allow me to purchase 10,000 shares, granted me by the company at a price that once sold will allow me to pay off the mortgage on the seaside cabin that I had struggled with for the last few months.

Giddy with my newfound wealth I decided to stop into my favorite watering hole before going home to announce the news to my family. As fortune would have it I ran into several of my buddies also having a pick me up, who was the loud mouth of the group, could tell that I was in high spirits that afternoon because I looked like the cat that swallowed the canary. He then implored me to divulge the good news. Bursting with feelings that equaled a Christmas Story, I blurted out the news of my companies new product. My buddies were duly impressed. On hindsight, I can only imagine what was going through their minds.

I believe that those of you that have a grasp of human nature know the ultimate answer. Each thought to themselves, let's check the bank account and buy as many share's as feasible.

My next stop was my impressive home where they all heard about my company's fortunate event, which caused dreams of sugarplums to form in their heads. Of course, this information did not stop there. Father and Mother Brothers and sisters, cousins, friends of friends and other's that had a need to know became "in the know."

So you see folks, many people will be buying this stock and driving up its price long before you hear about it. Most of them paid a very low price for this stock; consequently the downside for them is almost nil.

That will not be the case when you buy it. Appreciation in the share price of the company when it makes its debut may be as high as this company may see in its lifetime.

Bringing a product to market is time consuming and expensive. Depending on its pedigree, multiple hoops must be jumped. It's a good bet that the product will never see the light of day. The unlucky investor that came late to the party will be the first in line to get a haircut.

If you are thinking the Government has controls on insider trading, please calm yourself, and think again, it almost never happens that someone is charged with this horrifying offense. If they are, it's because they made a profit. But that's not you, Partner.

One of my tenets is to never act on purported insider information unless the CEO of the company is your father, and if that's the case you are a winner anyway.

As an adjunct to the foregoing, were you aware of the fact that currently serving members of Congress cannot be charged with insider trading. I'll leave it to you to figure that one out.

While you are figuring, have you noticed that legislators when elected live modestly? Of course, success is its own sensation. I have never personally witnessed a senator or congressman that failed. Failure in most cases would mean a decrease in your net worth. Am I not correct? That's not the case with our elected representatives. Year after year, their net worth increases. But where does this avalanche of money come from.

Well, let's do some more supposing. Suppose I own a company that makes a wonderful widget but that widget has to be made at a new facility that would be built in an environmentally sensitive area that has a species of fish on the endangered list.

A congressman from my district that has been a recipient of my largess in the past, just happened to be on the other end of an urgent phone call, heard me mention that the fish in question is now thriving according to a recent test carried out by a highly qualified firm in which I have a substantial interest. Of course the fish is no longer endangered and I can now proceed with the building of our grand new facility.

You may ask of course, how it was possible to get the necessary funds to my very close friend. There are laws that exist governing the amount of your political contribution. It seems that my company was about to report an abnormal profit and certainly my very close friend would benefit from the purchase on the open market of several thousand shares of my firm before earnings were announced to the general public.

The plant is built, carpenters and subcontractors of all types see their incomes increase, employment goes up, taxes to the various municipalities exceeds all expectations, unless the company has talked inexperienced politicians to forego taxes for the next ten years.

It seems that the city fathers relying on their innate intelligence decided this facility will be such an enhancement to the community, help in the way of $$$$$$ taken from the pockets of taxpaying citizens who never received tax relief for the next ten years like this company did, would be of great help to ensure the success of this venture.

So you see, everybody profits from this exercise of capitalism with maybe the exception being the tax paying public and possibly the fish.

I do not mean to be a burden on your psyche but I do want you to be aware that all those glitters may not be gold.

Be that as it may, you will still find plenty of gold lying around if you know where to look. I will be the director in the search for unbelievable stashes of green gold. So hang with me and concentrate. It will be so worth your time.

$ CHAPTER THREE $

The Search for Investments

If you have had an attitude adjustment then lets continue on. If you had to think about it, then we are not on the same book let alone the same page. However, if by telling the truth and destroying your fragile beliefs, I have made a new type investor out of you, than yea for me.

I am not foolish enough to believe that I will be able to change every person. As a matter of fact, if only a few people adhere to just some of the principles that I have laid out, I will have exceeded my expectations.

On the other hand, some bright enterprising fellow will come along and incorporate my wellspring of knowledge and other things he has been fortunate to acquire while inhaling knowledge gained from other sources and become more successful then I can imagine.

Finding Potential Investments

From this point, we will be interested in two types of securities; Stocks and options, derivatives of stocks.

There will not be a discussion of Real Estate, homes, land, and etcetera. Even though a plethora of money can be made in that area, it is not my sphere of expertise, plus not an easy way to make your fortune.

These are the stock exchanges we will be concerned with;

New York stock exchange Listed stocks 2,800. The most highly restricted exchange. Still uses specialists.

NASDAQ currently registered securities 3,100. The most active exchange. All trading is computerized.

American stock exchange referred to as the curb exchange. Trades a multitude of securities.

Occasionally I will refer to a stock being traded on the OTC or the Over the Counter market. Least restrictive exchange.

Advantages of the stock market and making your fortune on these exchanges.
    a) You are able to deal in securities around the world.
    b) Companies are constantly being listed.
    c) Your choice of thousands of companies to invest in.
    d) Instantaneous execution.
    e) Free flow of information.
    f) Favorable tax treatment.
    g) Work in your pajamas

Stocks come in all sizes and every imaginable profession, vocation, or enterprise that the mind can conceive. The price of its issue can vary from pennies to unaffordable heights. Some make excellent investments and some do not.

The task that we are undertaking is separating the wheat from the chaff, the good from the bad and not so bad. We must do it in a manner that is easy and not a quagmire of information that bogs down our search, resulting in indecisiveness and procrastination.

There are as many ways to check the basic value and future investable quality of a stock as there are professional analysts in the country, each with their own specialized method picking the right stock at the right time. Then why isn't everybody a millionaire? That is an easy question to answer. Only half or less of their picks will go up in the short term, but a majority will go up in the long term. So why don't we just hold for the long term?

Unfortunately life intrudes, especially if you are young. Have you noticed more divorces are among the young and as you age divorces are less frequent? Hormones and testosterone are raging, the younger you are the more you spend on entertainment, babies, children, homes, toys, travel, relocations, furniture, appliances, and incidentals too numerous to mention and automobiles. This reminds me of the guy who was asked for a payment on an overdue account. His response was as follows:

"Dear Sir

In reply to your request to send a check, I wish to inform you the present condition of my bank account makes this almost impossible. My shattered financial condition being due to federal laws, state laws, brothers-in-law, sisters-in-law and out-laws."

"Through these laws, I am compelled to pay a business tax, amusement tax, school tax. Water tax, light tax, sewer tax, liquor tax, sales tax, income tax, food tax, furniture tax, franchise tax and telephone tax.

I am required to get a business license, car license, operation license, truck license, driver's license, hunting license, fishing license, not to mention a marriage license, and a dog license."

"I am also required to contribute to every society and organization which the genius of man is capable of bringing to life, to women's relief, unemployment relief and gold diggers relief, also to every hospital and charitable institution in the area."

"For my own safety, I am required to carry health insurance, life insurance, fire insurance, tornado insurance, car insurance, Hurricane insurance, unemployment insurance, compensation insurance, and old age insurance."

"My business is so governed, that it is no easy matter to find out who owns it. I am expected, suspected, disrespected, summoned, fined, commanded, and compelled until I provide an inexhaustible supply of

money for every known need, deed, desire, or hope of the human race.

Simply because I refuse to donate to something or other, I am boycotted, talked about, lied about, held up, held down, and robbed, until I am almost ruined."

"I can tell you honestly that except for a miracle that happened, I would not be able to enclose this check. The wolf that comes to so many doors just had pups in my kitchen. I sold them and here is my money.

Brokenly yours;

I think that says it all."

Another conundrum. It would seem that an investment kept over a longer period of time would be the superior investment, but we must be cognizant, the money received from the sale of that security would be useful in a superior speculation. So while the current venture sleeps for an indefinite period of time a new asset just getting started on its run is now available.

Below is a chart showing a stock that is stagnating.

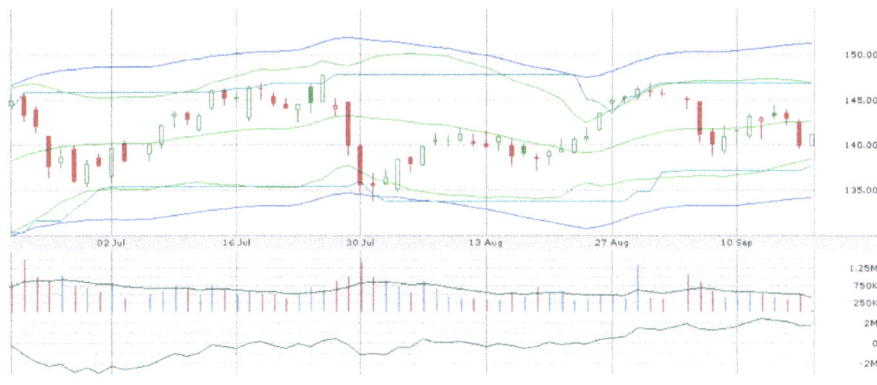

There is two glaring weaknesses this stock is exhibiting; the per share value is not showing an inclination to increase in value and the per share volume is declining. The meaning is clear; investors have loss interest in this security and any profits have been rung out. Why in the world would you hold it if there is about 15,000+ other stocks to peek at?

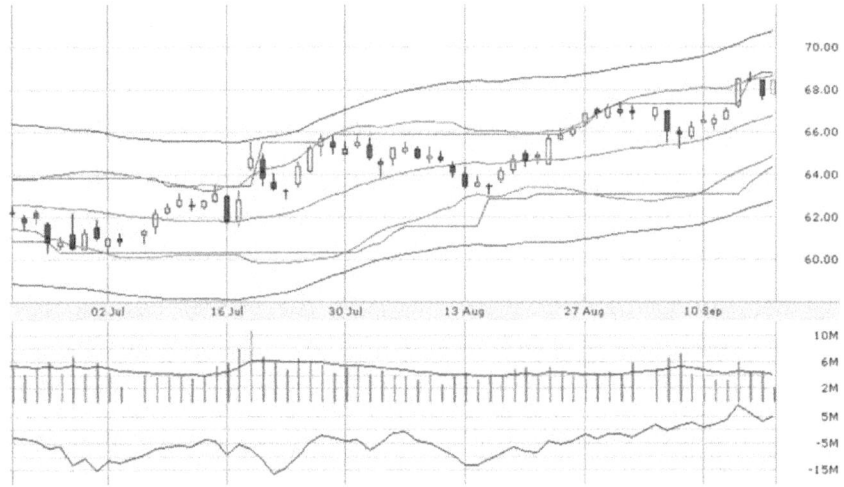

The chart above shows a stock that is moving in the proper direction. The per-share price has an upward momentum. A red flag; volume is squeezing. Would bear watching.

Valuation

The per share price that a stock is selling is called for our purposes valuation. Be it known that there are other types of valuations as an example; totaling the assets of a company minus liabilities is another type of valuation.

What does valuations mean to you; a simple explanation: assume company "A" has assets totaling 10,000 dollars and they issue stock and sell it at the value of the company, they could sell 10,000 shares for $1.00 each. However let's assume they issue only one share of stock, than we could expect that one share to sell for $10,000 dollars. So what does valuation mean to you? Absolutely nothing. If the value increases 10%, both shares would advance the same.

Valuation is to be considered as background noise and only in the context of other companies of the same ilk. In other words is the company we are considering the pick of the litter. Realize the most important consideration is the momentum of the stock price of the other company and companies under consideration. As nearly as possible express it in percentage terms, such as 10% per year or per quarter or whatever the number may be.

Remember that the price of the stock only reflects the sentiment of the buyers of the company. If there are more buyers than sellers the valuation increases and the reverse is true if there are more sellers than buyers. Keep in mind that an object that is in motion according to Newton's law tends to continue in that same direction.

Newton's laws of motion:

(General Physics) three laws of mechanics describing the motion of a body. The first law states that a body remains at rest or in uniform motion in a straight line unless acted upon by a force. The second law states that a body's rate of change of momentum is proportional to the force causing it. The third law states that when a force acts on a body due to another body, then an equal and opposite force acts simultaneously on that body.

The foregoing is a lot to swallow, just keep in mind a stock that's going up will have a tendency to continue in the same direction.

One must ask themselves, why is it going up? Is the "why" important to you? Not really. What is important; it's going up or down as the case may be, however in light of the fact that markets bias is an up direction. That is the bias of this book.

Utilizing Newton's second law a body's rate of change of momentum is proportional to the force causing it. In the case of stocks the forces behind the momentum is the top line (sales) and the bottom line (profits) which are the main driving forces, but not all the time, in many instances current news on a stock will overshadow sales and profits and of course news that is not generally known can be a great driver of momentum. And that brings us back to an old friend a conundrum, buy on the rumor and sell on the fact.

Oh, woe is me! What the hell do I do now. I know that's what some of you are saying. Yes, it's true, buying on the rumor doesn't always work. How about selling on the fact? Is that a true adage? No, it is not. Well than what is the truth? Sorry, there is no truth. But you could put together a few favorite things that will put the odds in your coroner and will enable you to occasionally land a haymaker or a few great jabs. If not a knockout you can still win on points.

The top line
This is the revenue line, the sales line, the heartbeat of the company. Without it, the company does not exist, at least as a viable entity.

The top line may mean something or nothing at all. Are sales accelerating, declining, or stagnating. If it is accelerating ask why and get an answer. How much is that line advancing year over year. Make sure the advance is in line with the bottom profit line percentage wise. If that is true, you may be looking at a winner. Assuming that this line is declining or possibly showing no inclination to rise from the floor, now we need to take a closer look at the reasons for its laconic state.

Next, look at the news on this stock. Is it favorable or negative or no news. This part requires some interpretation and future prognostication. Many times this information has no value to you if your expertise does not reach the level that is required for that particular product.

If all other aspects of this stock qualifies, than the news may not be significant and we can carry on.

The bottom line

This area of the investment is considered by many to be the all and the end all of any investment. Sorry to disappoint you, not true. Stay with me as I take you through the maze that we call statistics. The entire world of investing wants an investment that is earning substantial sums of money, including those that are looking for the next home run. Have you noticed that the very successful baseball home run hitters seem to strike out in an abnormal fashion? Quarterbacks in football will tend to have an incompletion record that does not favor the long aerial bombs that they throw. In golf the longer a competitor hits the ball generally misses more fairways. However in all cases they tend to be winners more often than not.

What does that tell us? It's not whispering it's yelling loudly, to investors looking for millions and not just a few dollars in dividends, the top line means more than the bottom line. Does that mean to completely ignore the bottom line? Not at all, the company you want is one that is going to grow its bottom line over a period of time to a substantial number in a reasonable amount of time. Remember no sales, no profits. The more sales now, the more profits down the road.

Realize dividends are not free. Stockholders pay dearly for those dividends. If you are long a position and that stock earns $1.00 a share and the company pays a .25-cent dividend, the entity that pays that dividend is you the shareholder. The value paid out in the form of dividends reduces the value of each share of stock. Now tell me, how does a paid dividend help me to increase my valuation? Not only that, but the dividend generally becomes a taxable event.

If a company is on a fast track and growing rapidly, every dime that comes in will be utilized and reinvested to improve the topline. We call that a growth stock. So what are we looking for? "Growth stocks!"

$ CHAPTER FOUR $

Finding Growth Stocks

If you have established an account through a reputable brokerage firm, they generally provide you with lists of stocks that they have vetted and placed in categories, i.e. high yield, conservative, large cap, small cap, growth, etc.

There are other places that willingly provide stocks in diverse classifications and are freely provided. In fact there are so many that you will be virtually inundated with choices.

Area's that interest us, are growth, large cap, small cap, and speculative.

As you peruse these lists find names that you may have a kissing relationship. Possibly general merchandise stores, factories where you have bought something from, drug chains, manufacturing plants, furniture, TV's, computer's, you get the idea. Having well-established companies such as Proctor and Gamble or McDonald's can be very comforting in your portfolio. Companies that pay a healthy dividend are also very comforting, however owning this type of investment will probably not bring in millions of dollars in compensation. A comprehensive list of high tech innovative companies can also be compiled this way. Settle on four or five, if you have the time look over a few more.

Look at their chart patterns, the one's that show a generally increasing pattern upward will be selected for further investigation. Be aware the construction of a chart can be misleading. A chart that has a steep upward progression may not be as significant as one that has a flatter trajectory. As time goes on you will have a practiced eye that gives immediate results.

So now you have settled on a few of these candidates for enshrinement in the hall of fame, find out exactly what they do. Companies can surprise you. What you thought they did may not be their major source of income. It is to your benefit to have an understanding of their role in business.

Your individual self comes to us packed with many biases, some are good some are bad and some occupy a semblance of neutrality. This book has not the time or the expertise to enhance or disparage your prejudices. I must make sure that they do not influence and get in the way of what we are trying to achieve, namely enhancing our pocketbook.

Knowing where a company gets most of its marble's gives us an inkling that we can juxtapose on to our understanding of life as we know it. This is where our judgement takes over and tells us if the product they are purveying is of importance as we see it.

Once you have decided on the company or companies you have selected, our next objective is to find out if anybody gives a damn about them. You can find this information on the bottom of most charts. It's the number of shares traded in a certain period of time, for instance one month, three months, six months. If the stock is trending upward with a corresponding increase in the volume of shares being traded, is a good indication this stock will probably continue on an upward path. If the reverse is true, it may be on its way downward.

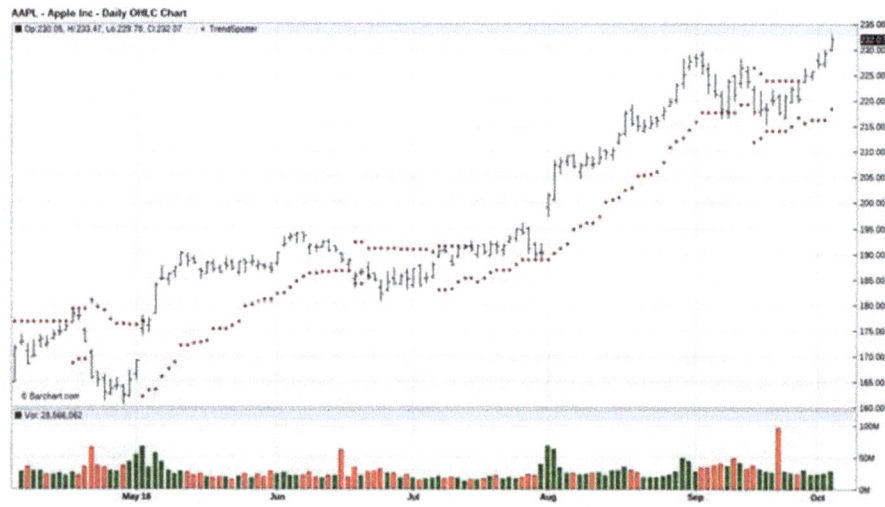

The above chart shows a stock moving in the proper direction.

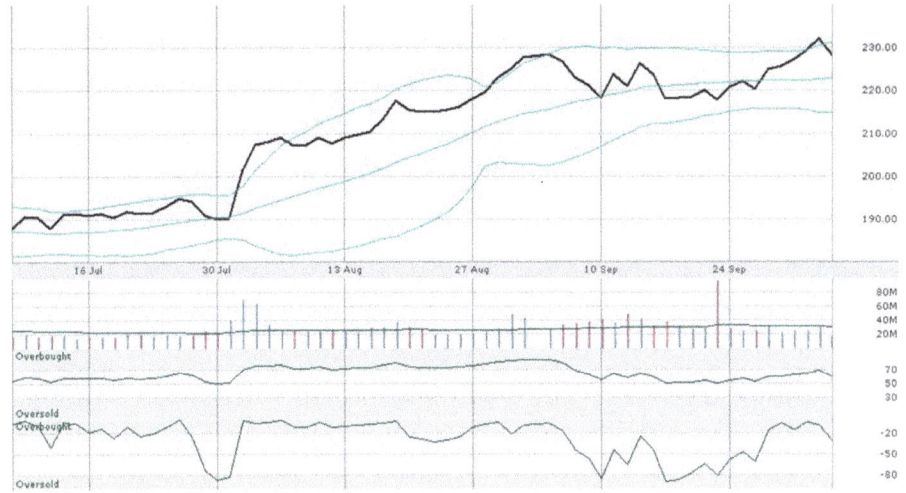

Chart showing Bollinger bands

In all scenarios, the prevailing wind may suddenly turn directions and that will happen inevitably in a certain percentage of the cases. Your impulse is directed by the amount of experience you have in charting and deciphering what the company does, its top line, bottom line, up or down volume and the direction and volatility in the trading and pricing of its shares. Another indicator we can use is called Bollinger bands. Make your own independent study of this indicator. It may help in your decision-making.

As an example; a stock we own trades at $22 each. Its variance for a few days is $22.50, $22.25, $ 21.90, $20.78 $19.99, now our experience and intuition takes over. Remember a few days does not a pattern of trading make. It's not just the pricing that matters it's the complete picture. All of the foregoing now comes into play. Eventually you will be able to make literally instantaneous decisions. It does not matter if you are right or wrong; action may be required.

The amount of inertia that takes place finally decides how much money comes to you. If you follow conventional wisdom; take your time; analyze each aspect of the trade ad nauseaum into infinity. If you are standing at the water's edge and don't move around you will slowly sink into the sand.

An incidence that transpired in my home brought this cornerstone to mind vividly. I had a friend and his wife invited that stayed for the weekend. Naturally, in the course of writing this book our conversation turned to investing. I knew him to be a consummate investor. During that weekend, he wanted to experience my methods. I gladly accommodated his request to use my method to help him in his quest to improve his selection of investments.

Sunday was spent brainstorming what we decided would be the securities to be taken advantage of Monday morning.

In this case we were looking at selling naked put options which are a derivative of particular stocks which I will cover in detail in this book. My friend departed early Monday morning traveling to their home in South Carolina.

As soon as trading began at 9:30 a.m. I immediately made the trades we had decided on the day before. Within a two-hour period, I had earned over nine hundred dollars, kept these investments for expiration in five days, and earned in excess of one thousand five hundred dollars. I called him later that week expecting to be congratulated and a thank you, but neither was forthcoming because he never executed the trades.

Believing he could get a better price, consequently he delayed taking advantage of an opportunity that was right in front of him. It was not just him but most people will trip over dollars to pick up nickels. It was not just the opportunity that was lost but his inability to see the bigger picture as more than likely many chances had been lost through his intransigence.

Examples of this type are legend, they are almost too numerous to mention.

My personal attorney who is also a close friend has a typical lawyer's attitude toward investing; he must know the final act before making a decision. This goes along with the lawyer's mantra; don't ask a question you don't already know the answer to. He loves animals especially dogs, so in the course of my rambling around the various offerings I found a stock that should make him happy.

The stock seemed to be an excellent growth factor with excellent product.

Freshpet, Inc. is a manufacturer of fresh, refrigerated pet food distributed across North America. The Company operates in the segment of manufacturing, marketing, and distribution of pet food and pet treats for dogs and cats. The Company's products consist of dog food, cat food, and dog and cat treats. Its recipes include real fresh meat and varying combinations of vegetables, leafy greens, and anti-oxidant rich fruits, without the use of preservatives, additives, or artificial ingredients. All of its products are sold under the Freshpet brand name, with ingredients, packaging, and labeling customized by class of retail. It also offers fresh treats across all classes of retail under the Dognation and Dog Joy labels. The Company's products are available in various forms, including slice and serve rolls, bagged meals and tubs. All of the Company's products are manufactured in the United States.

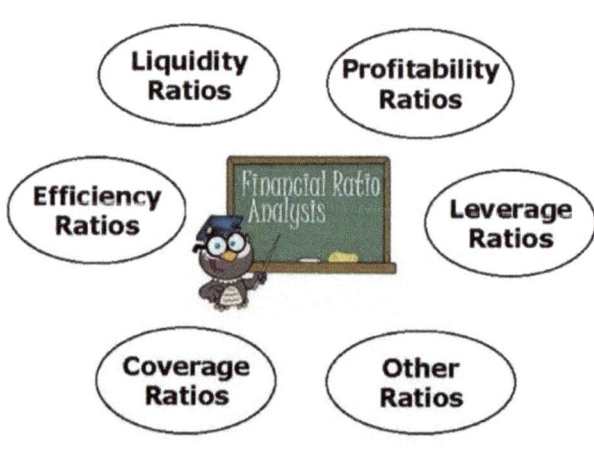

Price Performance since 2014
Low $5.60 - High $38.30

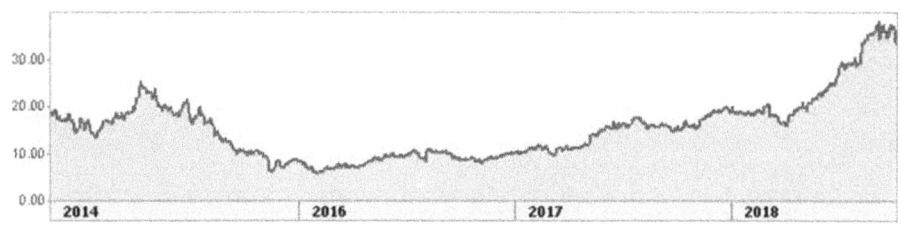

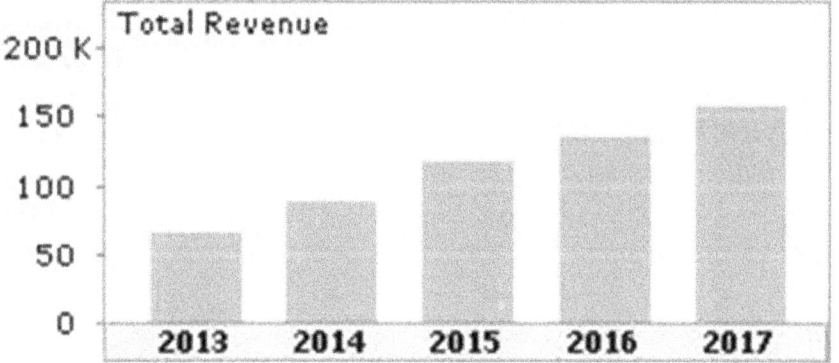

The above is a great example of a new growth story.

I would like to expound on the limitations to expansion this company has. Realize that it deals in fresh food for pets with no preservatives and no artificial ingredients, This means when selling to outlets they are asking for refrigerated shelf space which is limited, so it becomes a problem to the participating stores as to whether the product will generate enough income to justify occupying coveted refrigerated shelf space. Because of its specialized sector and loyal customer base this is not a problem.

I would point out that the company already has great branding and contracts in the food market area with major international corporations. It has created a moat around its product. That simply means competitors would be hard pressed to capture a significant foothold.

I included this lengthy example of Freshpet to show the importance of a company having a moat around it. This is not meant as a recommendation of the company. When selecting an investment do your own due diligence using the Cornerstones In this book or those that have become valuable to you over a period of time using your innate intellect coupled with experience.

Continuing with the gathering of stocks we may exploit, your brokerage will afford you with a compilation of sectors that have been performing well of late. Pick a couple of these that may interest you.

The first thing we will explore is their chart pattern. If it does not satisfy your standards, without further consideration erase it and do not consider it under any circumstances this is a bright red flag.

Do the offerings of this company appeal to you and do you think what this company is involved with, has a future. If so tuck it under your arm and let's continue.

One of the most important items is the amount of revenue this entity is generating. Is it increasing for a period of time percentagewise enough to satisfy you? That figure could be 5% 10% 20% or more. If it makes you happy than we have a go. A word of caution; if the increase that occurred in the revenue or profit was in the realm of fantasyland; it may be just a onetime thing and is not a pattern that we could rely on.

Profit should be in line with revenue except in the case of a new growing company where funds may be temporarily under water but the amount of deficit is less each year or quarter. Again the question is, does it satisfy you?

The next thing of some consequence, the amount of trading that is currently and recently occurring on the stock. If the price is rising and the trading is trending upward, a good sign and the reverse is also true. This may not eliminate the stock from consideration but it is a negative.

Entering a position is an art; never enter the full amount that is intended in one lump sum. Possibly 10 or 15 percent would be sufficient on the first entry, from there gradually move in until the amount meets your preconceived amount. Only keep buying if the intended investment is rising. Remember there can be too much of a good thing. If the velocity is too great in your estimation, than reprise your position.

If the action of the stock starts getting funky, by that I mean up, down, up, down, in other words not it's normal pattern; it may be time to start liquidating the position.

If the stock has gone negative 8 to 10 percent from its last high, sell it. Never take more than a 10 percent loss from its last high.

Again remember there are exceptions to any rule.

Never fall in love with a stock, because it will never love you back.

The hardest test you will face in your journey to being a millionaire or even a billionaire, when do I sell my position in a stock? There comes a time when everything ends.

The market has a wisdom all its own. No matter how good or bad things are such as rising or decreasing employment, the total economic scene, interest rates up or down or myriad other things that have an effect on market performance.

Remember that the United States is a world power so by necessity we will be involved in the international situation. Whatever is affecting other countries will affect our marketplace.

Every evening or morning make it a priority to know what the news of the day is. This can have an effect on your trading.

No matter how overbought or under bought the market is, it will at some point return to a more normal condition. If you have continued to buy in an overbought market when the correction takes place as it inevitably will, your losses could be dramatic. Markets tend to go down much faster than they go up. This is the point when your emotions take over and instead of taking a small loss you take a large capitation.

At the start of a correction it is not reasonable to assume how deep it will go. My suggestion is to exam all of your positions select the ones that are the biggest losers and start liquidating, possibly 25, 50, or even 75 percent. Keep in mind the assets now populating your portfolio have been at one point examined by you and found to be desirable. If the market turns around and starts another ascent, as it inevitably will, I may start reacquiring sold positions. Yes, it is true I may be buying at a higher price than I sold, and that's okay as long as they continue in the direction I want.

No matter what the prevailing opinion; it is not possible to buy at the lowest price and sell at the highest, unless you are extremely lucky and a miracle occurs, in most cases the person that promulgates that rhetoric is a liar or let's say has put lipstick on the truth.

This brings to mind a very interesting moment of enlightened enchantment with my wife. Many years ago, it seems I had discovered a sizzling stock. The symbol was CMGI, for the life of me I can't remember the name; however it was an internet company whose only claim to fame was bringing other small companies to market and initiated an IPO (initial public offering) which brought much wampum to the sponsoring company CMGI.

Startup internet companies were hot at the time and shares were in great demand, I recall purchasing the stock somewhere in the forties and purchasing a substantial number of shares for my wife's account and my account. Eventually the stock climbed to approximately $320 dollars a share. At that point my wife, not only greedier but many times wiser pointed to the fact that we had made a substantial sum of money on this situation so why not liquidate the position at $320. It was my position that I thought the company had a little more to run. I suggested not selling it at this time. In about a week the stock fell to about $300 and I changed my mind on the benefits of keeping this stock. I timidly approached my wife and suggested we sell at $300 and with my shares I did just that. She did not appreciate my suggestion in light of the fact that only a week ago we would have received $20 dollars more per share. I believe her intransigence in this matter was a case of greed.

The stock continued to fall and she stubbornly would not sell, believing the position would attain its former glory. Eventually she sold it at $11 and never mentioned this episode again. However from that point on when I made a suggestion, her answer was music to my ears "Do whatever you want" How many guys have ever heard that from their spouse? The stock is now called ModusLink Global Solutions and sells for $3 a share.

Trading methods of Jesse Livermore

1905 to 1941 Reiteration

1905 to 1941 Reiteration

I must apologize: the following was plagiarized from the book "Winners and Losers." It's okay. I was the author.

We finally come to the reason I might have a unique ability to analyze the trading systems of Jesse Livermore. My trading closely adheres to Jessie's with a radical exception I will cover later. First of all, is Jesse's system out of date? Not by a long shot, the difference is his approach to trading has come into the mainstream. What he called tape reading, we call charting. What took him hours or days to divine from tape reading, we do in a matter of seconds with computers. Insider trading is given to us almost immediately; what would have taken days to determine back then. News on a security is generally instantaneous, but not always. In this day and age, our tape is always running current, not lagging behind. Sometimes it was hours behind in Jesse's day.

To get an execution on one's trade in today's world is a matter of a few seconds. The cost of making a trade is much less today, hence the advent of the day trader. That would have been anathema in Jesse's day because of costs involved. Yet, the basic premise is still the same:

1) Determine the momentum of the general securities market. There are three kinds of movements that involve securities, Up, Down, Sideways.

2) Make a determination of the sectors that are reacting in the same direction as the general market.
3) Make a determination of the securities that are reacting in the same direction as the general market.
4) If a market is going in a sideways direction, Jesse would generally stay out of the market unless the tapes would be indicating through the volume and chart/tape pattern, that a general turn in this security was indicated.
5) Never take advice from other people.
6) Never yield to insider information
7) Do yourself a favor and be a lone wolf.
8) Volume, volume, volume, was Jesse's big obsession and for an excellent reason.
9) Volume was able to tell Jesse if a security was going up or down or getting ready for a transitional turn.
10) Remember, the market is more of an art than a science.
11) Learning to have a feel for the market, or security, is of overriding importance.
12) As you mature in your trading methods, volume will become more important to you and to your ability to beat the market.

Examples:
a) Stock that is riding higher on decreasing volume is probably going to start trending the other way, or getting ready to stagnate.

b) Stock that is trending higher on incremental increases in volume will, in all likelihood, go higher.
c) The reverse may be true. A stock that is going lower on incremental increases in volume is more likely to go lower.
d) Here is the catch. If a security has a sudden spike along with an increase in volume, either up or down in its trend, then that is called an exhaustion spike, or peak, and that security will now generally take a turn either up or down. The reason is that it has exhausted either the buyers or sellers in that security.
e) Notice that, in all cases, I have referred to the various different movements in a security with a connotation such as, generally, more than likely, probably, likelihood, or maybe. The reason is, the market has a peculiar way of reacting and having a mind of its own. Jesse only tried to put the prevailing odds in his favor.
13) Remember, being right all the time is impossible. The goal is being right 60% of the time.
14) Jesse, in most cases, liked to test a security before making a decisive move and he would invest small amounts. If the investment moved in the proper direction with strength, meaning volume and satisfactory movement of the price, either up or down, it would finally give him the conviction that he was correct in his assessment of that investment and he now would make a much larger outlay of capital.

15) Never allow a loss of greater than 10%. A favorite homily of mine that falls in the same category: Never fall in love with any investment because it will never love you back. HELL, IT WON'T EVEN NIBBLE ON YOUR EAR!
16) Absolutely do not listen to other investors that will try to tell you how truly great they are doing in the market. Always treat them as prevaricators and never allow dreams of sugarplums to dance in your head.

$ CHAPTER FIVE $

Short Sales

Now let's examine the other side; how can we make money in a down market. Can it be done? Yes it can but I'm not a proponent of that side of the bazaar. The exchange in its long history has had an upward bias. I must confess my bias is also upward. However there have been many successful investors that have made extraordinary profits selling short. One that comes to mind is Jessie Livermore who exceeded profits of 100 million in that devastating year 1929. At that time he was called the great bear of Wall Street. Because of his method of trading he created many enemies.

Too the uninitiated; a short sale occurs when a well-informed investor decides a particular stock will be declining in value. He borrows the number of shares he has deemed necessary with the intention of replacing them at some future date. He immediately sells those shares and for all intents and purposes pockets the money received with the objective of buying those shares at some future date of his choosing at his option and not the owner of those shares. Generally the brokerage house is the lending agent. The reason the brokerage has made this transaction is to increase commissions. The reason the investor has made this transaction is too potentially buy the shares at a lower price than he originally sold them.

A short sale can be lucrative if you have the expertise to determine the condition of a company. It may not be a liquidation of a business but possibly you believe its earnings are declining, so a short sale may be the expedient thing to do especially near that companies reporting date. One other indicator is the amount of shares being traded. If the volume is drying up, means that buyers are getting scarce, it's a red flag. Less buyers, more sellers, declining share price. Shorts happy, longs sad.

Let me reiterate short sales do not excite me. What does excite me is a hot Growth stock. Many of you place an undue reliance on the P/E ratio (profit to earnings ratio). Remember a growth stock will traditionally exhibit high P/E ratios. I vividly recall buying Amazon around $400 a share and liquidating a while later at something around $2,000 a share. I bought it when the P/E ratio was approximately 150 to one. At that time normal growth stocks were trading about 40 to one. I also remember holding Amazon when my total investment consisted of $400,000 dollars and knowing that stock was capable of dropping $100 points overnight made sleeping almost impossible, and so without further ado I liquidated enough shares to enable me to get a restful night's sleep.

Investing should not be stressful. Each person has their own level of anxiety they can handle with impunity. It's virtually impossible to make prudent decisions when tensions have taken over your life. When your portfolio is properly diversified you can easily ride out the bumps and blows you will inevitably experience. In your investing life, days of euphoria and dejection are normal. Remember the cornerstones that I have promulgated. Grab hold of persistence and tenacity and enjoy the ride because history is on your side.

Debt
Margin

The oldest adage in getting rich: "use other peoples money." Most of us use credit indiscrimanately, we use it to buy everything from groceries to cars and homes. Many of us carry only credit cards and no cash. Most of the things we buy are depreciating assets. People think of homes as an exellent investment. I beg to differ to some extent. When proudly selling our home for what we feel is an excellent profit, we conveintly forget to include in the cost of this home, insurance, repairs, pesticide treatment, yard enhancement, repairs that are a normal expense and modernization to keep up with the Jonse's, plus tools, (lawnmower, garden implements etc.) not to mention various forms of taxes and interest on the mortgage. For the most part our society impales us with excessive amounts of interest on debt that has no advantages of accellerating our networth.

Margin, is a loan provided to you by your brokerage company. If used wisely it is a perk that has many benefits. The most beneficial benefit increases your leverage amount by at least 50% at a competitive rate of interest.

One creavet; your portfolio must have enough unencombered assets to give the brokerage company protection in the event your investment takes a turn into a bottomless pit.

The use of Stops

There are three types of stop losses:

1. A stop market, allows you to name a price that you have decided is a price that you are willing to accept to sell your position. The catch to be aware of, as with anything in the market, that's not necessarily the price you will receive. The price you have indicated is simply the price that is activated when the market falls to that level. The price you will actually receive is the next prevailing price that is bid. (market order)
2. A stop limit is simply the price and the only price you will accept, which means if the stock never trades at that particular price, you will not have a transaction on your position.
3. A trailing stop, an interesting anomaly that allows you to pick in percentage terms the price your position will decline from its high and your indicated price than becomes a market order and is sold at the next prevailing bid price to receive activation.

I personally am not captivated using stops except I believe a trailing stop can make a lot of sense if you are not able to be in constant contact with your portfolio. In many cases when a stop is manifested, it leaves you in an unsatisfied position.

Far too many times, I have seen a stop activated at a loss during a day's trading and while fluctuating touch your stop only to see that stock start an extended rise. Remember that position was selected based on proper intelligence, the corollary is an expectation of profit. The exception in most cases is a loss of 10% making a dumping of some of the shares necessary.

When entering or leaving a position.
My preferred method of buying into a new investment is slowly with a judgement based upon the amount I am willing to commit in total to that particular position.

Let's assume that my amount at the moment I enter will be an intended 1,000 shares. My first buy may be only two hundred shares, which gives me a chance to determine the action of the stock. If it continues to meet my expectations, I may invest another 400 and again based on the action of the stock I may eventually reach my gratification level. That level will inevitably change depending on circumstances. Once again we should be depending on experience level, the news on that stock and the general news of the day.

Factor in what the president and the congress are up to in that time period and let's not forget the Federal Reserve. Dig up the statistics on sectors which can give insight what is favorable or not.

Regardless of the foregoing if your glamorous beauty of the moment is not giving out the required buying signals, even though you have not completed your intended buying, the reverse may take place, and selling in increments is now the order of the day. So remember, when we have become disenchanted with a particular entity, we sell in increments until we have a change in attitude based on various factors that I have previously covered.

Always remember that my proclivity is momentum. Even though other factors are involved, Momentum one-way or the other takes precedent.

At this point I must interject a very important subject that has an immense effect on our lives in America and worldwide.

It is important to have at least a nodding knowledge of the;

"Federal Reserve"

It is not necessary to read the following on the Fed if you have even a minor understanding of what the Fed does and know that it has a wide-ranging effect on your investments.

Read it if you want to be really smart.

Updated December 12, 2018
The Federal Reserve and What It Does
How the Fed Affects Your Life Every Day

The Federal; reserve system is America's central bank that makes it the most powerful single actor in the U.S. economy and thus the world. It is so complicated that some consider it a "secret society" that controls the world's money. They're right. Central banks do manage the money supply around the globe. But there is nothing secret about it.

System Structure

To understand how the Fed works, you must know its structure. The Federal Reserve System has three components. The Board of Governors directs monetary policy. Its seven members are responsible for setting the discount rate and the reserve requirement for member banks. Staff economists provide all analyses. They include the monthly Beige Book and the semi-annual Monetary Report to Congress.

The Federal Open Market Committee oversees open market operations. That includes setting the target for the fed funds rate, which guides interest rates. The board members and four of the 12 bank presidents are members. The FOMC meets eight times a year.

The Federal Reserve Banks supervise commercial banks and implement policy. They work with the board to supervise commercial banks. There is one located in each of their 12 districts.

What the Federal Reserve Does

The Federal Reserve has four functions. It's most critical and visible function is to manage inflation and maintain stable prices. It sets a 2 percent inflation target for the core inflation rate. Why is managing inflation so important? Ongoing inflation is like an insidious cancer that destroys any benefits of growth.

Second, the Fed supervises and regulates many of the nation's banks to protect consumers. Third, it maintains the stability of the financial markets and constrains potential crises. Fourth, it provides banking services to other banks, the U.S. government, and foreign banks.

The Fed performs its functions by conducting monetary policy. The goal of monetary policy is healthy economic growth. That target is a 2 to 3 percent gross domestic product growth rate. It also pursues maximum employment. The goal is the natural rate of unemployment of 4.7 to 5.8 percent.

Manages Inflation

The Federal Reserve controls inflation by managing credit, the largest component of the money supply. This is why people say the Fed prints money. The Fed moderates long-term interest rates through open market operations and the fed funds rate.

When there is no risk of inflation, the Fed makes credit cheap by lowering interest rates.

This increases liquidity and spurs business growth. That ultimately reduces unemployment. The Fed monitors inflation through the core inflation rate, as measured by the Personal Consumer Expenditures Price Index. It strips out volatile food and gas prices from the regular inflation rate. Food and gas prices rise in the summer and fall in the winter. That's too fast for the Fed to manage.

The Federal Reserve uses expansionary monetary policy when it lowers interest rates. That expands credit and liquidity. These make the economy grow faster and create jobs. If the economy grows too much, it triggers inflation. At this point, the Federal Reserve uses contractionary monetary policy and raises interest rates. High-interest rates make borrowing expensive. Increased loan costs slow growth and decrease the likelihood of businesses raising prices. The major players in the fight against inflation are the Federal Reserve chairs.

These are the heads who manage the Fed's interest rates.

The Fed has many powerful tools. It sets the reserve requirement for the nation's banks. It states that banks must hold at least 10 percent of their deposits on hand each night. This percentage is less for smaller banks. The rest can be lent out.

If a bank doesn't have enough cash on hand at the end of the day, it borrows what it needs from other banks. The funds it borrows is known as the fed funds. Banks charge each other the fed funds rate on these loans.

The FOMC sets the target for the fed funds rate at its monthly meetings. To keep it near its target, the Fed uses open market operations to buy or sell securities from its member banks. It creates the credit out of thin air to buy these securities. This has the same effect as printing money. That adds to the reserves the banks can lend and results in the lowering of the fed funds rate. Knowledge of the current fed funds rate is important because this rate is a benchmark in financial markets.

Supervises the Banking System

The Federal Reserve oversees roughly 5,000 bank holding companies, 850 state bank members of the Federal Reserve Banking System, and any foreign banks operating in the United States. The Federal Reserve Banking System is a network of 12 Federal Reserve banks that both supervise and serve as banks for all the commercial banks in their region.

The 12 banks are located in Boston, New York, Philadelphia, Cleveland, Richmond, Atlanta, Chicago, St. Louis, Minneapolis, Kansas City, Dallas, and San Francisco. The Reserve Banks serve the U.S. Treasury by handling its payments, selling government securities, and assisting with its cash management and investment activities. Reserve banks also conduct valuable research on economic issues.

The Dodd-Frank Wall Street Reform Act strengthened the Fed's power over banks. If any bank becomes too big to fail, it can be turned over to Federal Reserve supervision. It will require a higher reserve requirement to protect against any losses.

Dodd-Frank also gave the Fed the mandate to supervise "systematically important institutions." In 2015, the Fed created the Large Institution Supervision Coordinating Committee. It regulates the 16 largest banks. Most important, it is responsible for the annual stress test of 31 banks. These tests determine whether the banks have enough capital to continue making loans even if the system falls apart as it did in October 2008.

On February 3, 2017, President Trump attempted to weaken Dodd-Frank. He signed an executive order that instructed the Treasury Secretary to review areas that need to be amended. But many of those regulations have already been incorporated into international banking agreements.

Maintains the Stability of the Financial System

The Federal Reserve worked closely with the Treasury Department to prevent global financial collapse during the financial crisis of 2008. It created many new tools, including the Term Auction Facility, the Money Market Investor Lending Facility, and Quantitative Easing. For a blow-by-blow description of everything that happened while it was going on, the article discussing federal intervention in the 2007 banking crisis gives a clear account.

Two decades earlier, the Federal Reserve intervened in the Long Term Capital Management Crisis. Federal Reserve actions worsened the Great Depression of 1929 by tightening the money supply to defend the gold standard.

Provides Banking Services

The Fed buys U.S. Treasury's from the federal government. That's called monetizing the debt. The Fed creates the money it uses to buy the Treasury's. It adds that much money to the money supply. Over the past 10 years, the Fed has acquired $4 billion in Treasury's.

The Fed is called the "bankers' bank." That is because each Reserve bank stores currency, processes checks, and makes loans for its members to meet their reserve requirements when needed. These loans are made through the discount window and are charged the discount rate, one that is set at the FOMC meeting. This rate is lower than the fed funds rate and Libor. Most banks avoid using the discount window because there is a stigma attached. It is assumed the bank can't get loans from other banks. That's why the Federal Reserve is known as the bank of last resort.

History

The Panic of 1907 spurred Congress to create the Federal Reserve System. It established a National Monetary Commission to evaluate the best response to prevent ongoing financial panics, bank failures, and business bankruptcies. Congress passed the Federal Reserve Act of 1913 on December 23 of that year.

Congress originally designed the Fed to "provide for the establishment of Federal Reserve banks, to furnish an elastic currency, to afford means of rediscounting commercial paper, to establish a more effective supervision of banking in the United States, and for other purposes." Since then, Congress has enacted legislation to amend the Fed's powers and purpose.

Congress created the Fed's board structure to ensure its independence from politics. Board members serve staggered terms of 14 years each. The president appoints a new one every two years. The U.S. Senate confirms them. If the staggered schedule is followed, then no president or congressional party majority can control the board.

This independence is critical. It allows the Fed to focus on long-term economic goals. It can make all decisions based solely on economic indicators. No president can pressure members to keep interest rates low and overstimulate the economy.

President Trump is the first president in history to question that independence. In 2018, he publicly criticized the Fed for raising interest rates. He said higher rates slow growth and offset his attempts to spur the economy. When asked to name the single greatest threat to growth, he blamed the Fed.

This is despite the fact that Trump nominated six of the seven members. The Senate has confirmed three of them. Trump inherited this rare opportunity to stack the Fed board in his favor. The chair position came up for reappointment during his term. Three board positions were already vacant, including the vice-chair position. Two of them have been vacant since the financial crisis.

Who Owns the Fed

Technically, member commercial banks own the Federal Reserve. They hold shares of the 12 Federal Reserve banks. But that doesn't give them any power because they don't vote. Instead, the Board and FOMC make the Fed's decisions. The Fed is independent because those decisions are based on research. The president, U.S. Treasury Department, and Congress don't ratify its decisions. But, the board members are selected by the president and approved by Congress. That gives elected official's control over the Fed's long-term direction but not its day-to-day operations.

Some elected officials are still suspicious of the Fed and its ownership. They want to abolish it all together. Senator Rand Paul wants to control it by auditing it more thoroughly. His father, former Congressman Ron Paul, wanted to end the Fed.

Role of the Fed Chair

The Federal Reserve Chair sets the direction and tone of both the Federal Reserve Board and the FOMC. President Trump appointed Board member Jerome Powell to be the chair from February 5, 2018, to February 5, 2022. He is continuing the Fed's normalizing policies.

The former chair is Janet Yellen. Her term began on February 3, 2014, and ended on February 3, 2018. Her biggest concern had been unemployment, which is also her academic specialty. That made her "dovish" rather than "hawkish." That meant she was more likely to want to lower interest rates. Ironically, she was the chair when the economy required contractionary monetary policy.

Ben Bernanke was the chair from 2006 to 2014. He was an expert on the Fed's role during the Great

Depression. That was very fortunate. He knew the steps to take to end the Great Recession. He kept the economic situation from turning into a depression.

How the Fed Affects You

The press scrutinizes the Federal Reserve for clues on how the economy is performing and what the FOMC and Board of Governors plan to do about it. The Fed directly affects your stock and bond mutual funds and your loan rates. By having such an influence on the economy, the Fed also indirectly affects your home's value and even your chances of being laid off or rehired.

Summing Up

1) Start an exploration of stocks:
2) Look at the Chart, is the trend what you want
3) Check volume. Many times volume can tell you if a stock is going up or down on strength or whether a strong turn is in its future.
4) Be acutely aware of the news of the day and how it will affect your choices in the market.
5) Remember the top line of a company is the revenue line. The most essential and influential statistic that you have.

Your broker will provide you with an array of choices.

My personal choice is TD Ameritrade but there are many other quality brokerage firms. Follow me as I select stocks that I will cull from their web dated 12/1/2018. A tab appears with the moniker "Research and Ideas" under that section you will find a list of sectors and other statistics pertaining to their performance in that week.

A very tough week and month for the market.

China was unrelenting in subscribing to unfair methods of trade in this period.

Communication Services

The Communication Services sector was up 0.23% Friday, with 3 out of 5 of its underlying industries gaining. Interactive Media & Services was the strongest industry, rallying by 1.13%. Over the last month, the Communication Services sector is unchanged. Diversified Telecommunication Services and Wireless Telecommunication Services are the best performing, returning 3.84%, and 2.43% respectively.

I selected a stock from a list offered by TD Ameritrade:

Quinstreet Inc. (QNST)

16.14 +0.46 (+2.93%) 11/30/18 [NASDAQ]
Quote Overview for Fri, Nov 30th, 2018
Day Low
15.48
Day High
16.22
Open 15.65
Previous Close 15.68
Volume 1,138,500
Avg Vol 900,380
Stochastic %K 52.65%
Weighted Alpha +44.54
5-Day Change +1.49 (+10.17%)
52-Week Range 8.24 - 17.75

The very first thing that should draw your attention is its chart pattern and volume.

Below is the three-month chart.

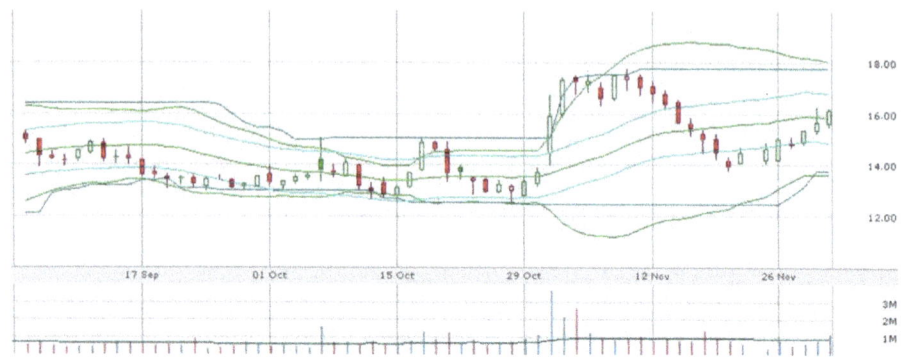
Volume

This chart shows this stock giving indications of wanting to advance as confirmed by the volume chart. Notice volume spiked as the stock spiked and as it declined volume dried up.

Revenue

This area was nothing to brag about. Very uneven.

Financial Statements

(Values displayed are in thousands)

Balance Sheet

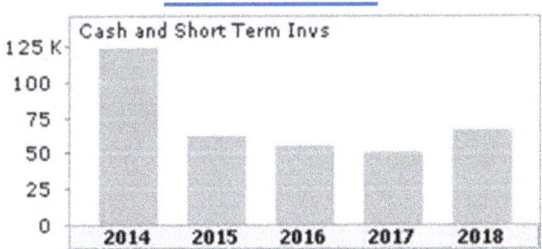

Income Statement

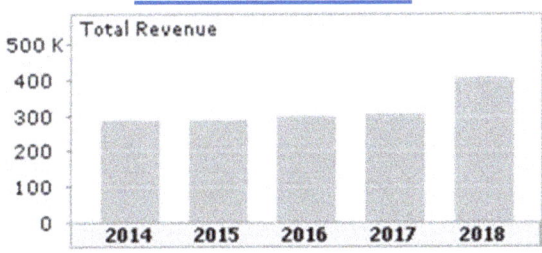

Cash Flow

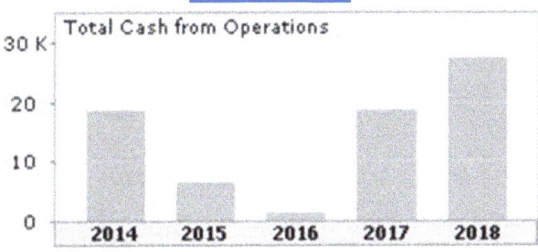

Values displayed are in thousands. Cash flow has little interest to me.

Insider Trading

During the most recent quarter, 2M shares were sold in insider trading. Many traders place a great deal of emphasis on insider trading. I believe in most cases it has very little value. I give passing notice if any.

If the directors of a company had a clue to what the company would do in the future, everyone would be immensely wealthy. We know that all the officials of an enterprise are generally well off but certainly not in any way off the charts.

What actually goes on in the innards of a company? Generally directors and others that are not involved in the day-to-day operation are not highly compensated. Instead they receive a stipend in the form of stock options. Others that are an integral part of the organization are also awarded options that they automatically receive as part of their compensation.

Eventually these options are converted and sold on the prevailing exchange. So when you look at published numbers of insider selling they are mostly compensation to employees of the company.

Remember officers and other highly paid individuals have the same problems that we all have; pay on the mortgage, the new car, the latest divorce, child support, their girlfriend's dentist and other appropriations too numerous to mention.

Do not be hypnotized by the number on insider trading. It's just something to be aware of. However if the numbers have a relevance beyond what you think should be in a proper range, than give it some credence.

As an aside, all of those shares tend to dilute the shares you are holding.

Earnings
Latest Earnings Beat Consensus (Q1 ending 09/2018)
Next Earnings Announcement

Q1 Non-GAAP Earnings 10/30/2018	Q1 Consensus .14 of 6 Analysts	Difference .13 consensus		Q2 10.71 will announce	Unconfirmed 01/29/2019

Quarterly Earnings History and Estimates

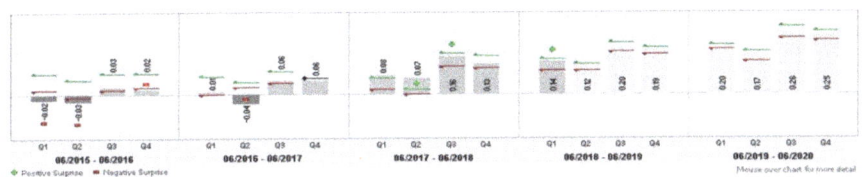

**My synopsis of this stock in a nutshell is NO!!!
There is very little to recommend.
Uneven in every aspect.**

Take note of the fact that TD Ameritrade recommended this stock.

There's no one perfect way to beat the market. Some traders prefer highflying growth stocks, while others prefer deeply discounted value stocks. Some may prefer fast-paced momentum stocks, whereas others are more comfortable with mature, dividend producing income stocks.

The most powerful wealth provider in the world "the stock market" can be beat in a variety of ways.

I will always be on the side of momentum, an investment that is trending up and does not look back, at least not in the near future. Buying a discounted stock on its way down is like catching a falling knife. No thanks! Buying a dividend payer is like watching paint dry.

If you must be ultra conservative with your funds than try bank CD's and hope you don't die before you earn a few pennies.

I would suggest spending your nights curled up in front of the fireplace reading a good novel. Forget the stock market; it may hasten your death from a heart attack. Of course on the other hand investing in CD's may hasten your death from boredom.

Let's look at another stock shall we? Hopefully it will be a better selection.

New Age Beverages Corp NASDAQ: NBEV
Consumer Staples: Beverages, Small Cap Growth
Company profile

The New Age Beverage Corporation, formerly Bucha, Inc., is a healthy functional beverage company. The Company is the owner of XingTea, XingEnergy, Aspen Pure and the Bucha Live Kombucha brands. The Company's bucha Live Kombucha is a gluten free, organic certified, sparkling kombucha tea and is distributed in health and grocery chains across North America. The Company offers its bucha Live Kombucha products in approximately 16-ounce bottle. The Company offers XingTea in approximately 13 flavors. Its product, XINGjuice, is a natural juice drink, made with cane sugar and real fruit juice. Its product, XingEnergy is a naturally flavored cane sugar product. The Company's product, Aspen Pure, is bottled water packaged in approximately 24-ounce, half-liter, and one-liter bottles. The Company offers products in approximately 46 states within the United States and in over 10 countries internationally across all channels through direct and store door distribution systems.

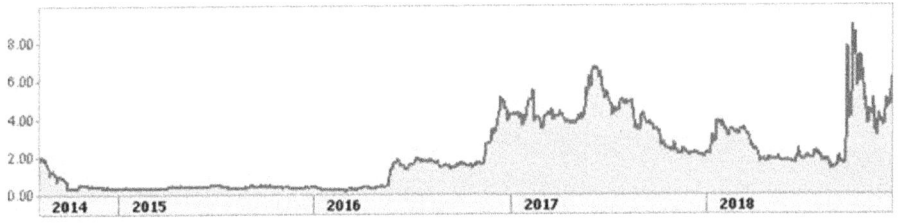

Researched on 12/12/2018 price $6.15
1) The chart does nothing for me however the market at this time has been extremely volatile, so I have made an exception in this case.

2) I am captivated by it's in vogue current products and the possibilities of the explosion of the THC infused drinks market that could be in its future.
3) Stock price has advanced 80% in the last 30 days. This may be a red flag. Care must be taken. Traders may be in the mood to take profits.
4) Even though I am not in favor of stops, in this case I would use a 15% trailing stop.
5) Volume is not favorable.
6) If you elect to purchase this stock realize at best it will be a short-term venture.
7) In my opinion I would buy it and stay with it until the price action indicates that a sale should be eminent. An indicator would be a chart pattern of lower lows and lower highs.

   On this stock it would be a good idea to be impatient and quick to pull the trigger.

The foregoing stocks are examples of the things you should look for in acquiring a new investment.

Most of the time stock evaluation can be done using a few simple directives'.

1) Generally inclining chart, enough to satisfy your expectations.
2) Increasing revenue over the last few years. (The top line).
3) Profit, increasing incrementally each year, potentially a mirror of revenue, but not necessarily. A quickly growing new Corp. may take time to match profit to the top line.
4) Volume should be increasing when the stock price is rising. Doing the opposite is a strong red flag.

The foregoing stock or stocks, is purely an example only and not a recommendation.

Again remember to use your own intelligence that will become more enhanced as you acquire greater experience.

Bear Markets

Financial Definition of a bear market
What It Is - A bear market is a period of several months or years during which securities prices consistently fall. The term is typically used in reference to the stock market, but it can also describe specific sectors such as real estate, bond, or foreign exchange. It is the opposite of a bull market, in which asset prices consistently rise.
How It Works

Identifying and measuring bear markets are both art and science. One common measure says that a bear market exists when at least 80% of all stock prices fall over an extended period. Another measure says that a bear market exists if certain market indexes -- such as the Dow Jones Industrial Average and the S&P 500 -- fall at least -15%. Of course, different market sectors may experience bear markets at different times.

The bear market that occurred in the U.S. equity markets from 1929 to 1933 is one of the most notorious bear market in history.

The causes and characteristics of bear markets vary, but most financial theorists agree that economic cycles and investor sentiment both play a role in the creation and momentum of bear markets. In general, a weak or weakening economy -- indicated by low employment, low disposable income, and declining business profits, together with a lack of capital -- ushers in a bear market.

The existence of several new trading lows for well-known companies might also indicate that a bear market is occurring. It is important to note that government involvement affects bear markets. Changes in the federal funds rate or in various tax rates can encourage economic expansion or contraction, ultimately leading to bull or bear markets.

Falling investor confidence is perhaps more powerful than any economic indicator, and it also often signals a bear market. When investors believe something is going to happen (a bear market, for example), they tend to take action (selling shares in order to avoid losses from expected price decreases), and these actions can ultimately turn expectations into reality. Although it is a difficult measure to quantify, investor sentiment shows through in mathematical measurements such as the put/call ratio, the advance/decline line, IPO activity and the amount of outstanding margin debt.

Regardless of their exact beginnings and ends, bear markets typically have four phases. In the first phase, prices and investor sentiment are high, but investors are beginning to take profits and exit the market. In the second phase, stock prices begin to fall quickly, trading activity increases and corporate earnings fall, and positive economic indicators are below average. Investor sentiment also gets more pessimistic and some investors panic. Market indices and many securities reach new trading lows, trading activity continues to increase, and dividend yields reach historic highs. In the third phase, prices and trading volume increase somewhat as speculators enter the market. In the fourth and final phase, stock prices continue to fall, but they do so at a slower pace. As investors find prices low enough and as they react to good news or positive indicators, bear markets often eventually give way to bull markets.

Why It Matters: Bear markets cost investors' money because security prices generally fall across the board.

But bear markets don't last forever, and they don't always give advance notice of their arrival. The investor must know when to buy and when to sell to maximize his or her profits. As a result, many investors attempt to "time the market," or gauge when a bear market has begun and when it is likely to end.

Analysts spend thousands of hours trying to mathematically determine what will trigger the next bear market and how long it will last, and technical analysis is especially prevalent in this effort.

Following my suggestions; lighten your portfolio as the market declines by gradually selling a percentage and keeping a percentage of a well-researched stock which will put you in a position to lessen the impact of a declining market and improves your stance when a bull market reappears and you gradually start reacquiring previously sold shares. In all cases when a position starts to fall apart, exam your previous assumptions you had originally held, to ascertain if anything has changed.

To amplify the previous statement assume you held 100 shares of a stock at $200 a share. When the market starts to decline you liquidated 25 shares at $190 for a loss of $250. As it declines another $10, another 25 shares are sold, your loss on that 25 becomes $500 and yet again it declines another $10, 25 more shares are sold at $170 a loss of $750, it eventually bottoms out at $150. In the above scenario you sold 75 shares for a loss of $1500 plus a loss of $50 a share on the 25-share position that you are still holding at a value of $150 or a loss of $1250. Total loss on the total situation in the portfolio becomes $2750 if you would have held the entire position riding it down to $150 your loss becomes $5000 instead of $2750 a difference of $2250. To put it in percentage terms it becomes a savings of 45% calculated on the original 100 shares.

Well, just imagine that! You thought it was a loss, but low and behold it was a savings of 45%. Now you know what magic is.

If your original projection was correct, at some point the shares you hold will start reversing. Now, instead of selling you would become a buyer and restore your original 100 shares doing it in increments satisfactory to you, or possibly more if the trajectory is strong enough.

One general indicator of a bear market; if your neighbor's portfolio falls by 15% that is not a bear market. If your portfolio falls by 15%, that is a catastrophic bear market.

For those of you that do not have a well-developed sense of humor, the preceding statement was meant to be facetious.

$ CHAPTER SIX $

Options

 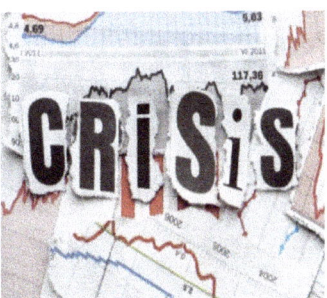

Get ready here come the Dreaded Derivatives

Options are simply gambling on the price of what we call the underlying stock, investment, security, or asset. In other words the core investment that exercises' control over the option.

In this part of the learning curve, we will enter a realm that is completely foreign to most investors. Even experienced traders in many instances lack expertise in this area. I have undertaken a very simple approach to investing in options called **KISS** which is the acronym of **keep it simple stupid.**

Follow me along as I unfurl the terms that are commonly used by those who express a condescending attitude toward those that are neophytes in the option game, commonly shown to those investors that were never grounded in the vicissitudes of the option experience.

Terms that is commonly used:
1) ATM = At the money
2) OTM = Out of the money
3) VOL = Implied volatility
4) LONG = Place trade for a debit
5) SHORT = place trade for a credit
6) CLASS = Types of option i.e. Call or Put

Terms not so commonly used and how to use them:
1) **Long Butterfly**

How?
    Buy 1 ATM option (calls or puts)
    Buy 2 further out OTM options (calls or puts)
    Buy one further out OTM option (same class)

Why?
Slightly directional defined-risk, bet the stock lands near the short strike you think stock will be near at

expiration. Losses will likely occur when stock moves outside of the expected range.
When?
Consider when high volatility pushes down their prices and you think the stock will move to a specific price and no more.

2) **Short call vertical**

How?
    Sell ATM or OTM call
    Buy further out OTM

Why?
Defined-risk and defined-profit. High volatility increases price of OTM verticals. Fine-tune risk and reward by widening or narrowing strikes. Max loss can occur when stock price falls below long strike prior to or at expiration.

When?
Volatility is high and you think stock will trade neutral to lower at expiration.

2) **Short Strangle**
How?
    Sell one OTM put
    Sell one OTM call

Why?

Undefined risk strategy designed to profit from time decay and decreasing volatility as stock remains in an expected range. Without hedges, credit is larger than iron condor, but the potential for significant loss is more substantial due to the unlimited loss potential of the uncovered call position.

When?

High volatility expected to fall. For larger accounts that have the necessary capital, higher risk tolerance.

3) Short put vertical

How?

  Sell ATM or OTM put
  Buy further out OTM put

Why?

Defined risk and defined profit. High vol increases price of OTM verticals. Fine tune risk and reward by widening or narrowing strikes. Maximum low can occur when stock price falls below long strike prior to or at expiration.

When?

Vol is high and you think stock will trade neutral to higher at expiration.

4) **Iron Condor**
How?
   Sell one OTM put vertical
   Sell one OTM call vertical
   Why?
   Defined risk bet designed to profit from time decay and decreasing volatility if stock remains in an expected range. Should stock move substantially. Losses can occur.

When?
   High vol expected to fall. Higher vol means higher credits. Larger potential profit, and smaller risk.

5) **Long calendar**

How?
   Buy longer-term ATM option
   Sell shorter-term ATM option

Why?
   Defined risk bet on the stock landing near short strike at option expiration. Can benefit from low or rising volatility. Look for roughly equal vol between short and long options. Losses can occur when volatility falls in long strike or stock trades out of expected range at expiration of short strike.

When?

Volatility is low (reduces debits of calendars) and stock expected to trade in a range.

At this point most of you are completely non-plused at the seeming complexity of the names of the various types of option variables which in the end don't mean a damn thing.

While we are into damn things, let's let the other shoe drop. Have you ever heard of "Geeks?" Sometimes referred to as Greeks No, I'm not talking about your brother or even your friends. No, I'm still talking about options.

In options trading, you may notice the use of certain Greek alphabets when describing risks associated with various positions. They are known as "the Greeks."

Options Geeks and Market Geeks were both founded by Roger Scott, a hedge fund manager, professional trader, and a successful entrepreneur with many years of experience in the financial markets industry. About 1990, not that long ago.

In mathematical finance, the Geeks are the quantities representing the sensitivity of the price of derivatives such as options to a change in underlying parameters on which the value of an instrument or portfolio of financial instruments is dependent. The name is used because the most common of these sensitivities are denoted by Greek letters (as are some other finance measures).

There are four of them, as follows:
1) Delta=a measure of an options sensitivity to changes in the price of the underlying asset.
2) Gamma=is a measure of delta's sensitivity to changes in the price of the underlying asset.
3) Vega=is a measure of an option's sensitivity to changes in the volatility of the underlying asset.
4) Theta=is a measure of an option's sensitivity to time decay.

And guess what? There are other ways of measuring and choosing an option, for instance the Black Scholes method.

The Black Scholes Merton model is a mathematical model of a financial market containing derivative investment instruments.

There are six pricing variables in this method.
1) Implied volatility
2) Type of option
3) Underlying stock price
4) Time value
5) Strike price
6) European calls and puts

A study of this model can prove to be beneficial. However its importance is relative to your basic nature. Some personalities are perfectionate in nature and others tend to be a little more relaxed and yet others are always in a hurry. Each has its good omens and bad omens.

Learn to deal with your traits. Allow the good to outweigh the bad. I believe the type of individual reading this manuscript, has a comprehension level greater than most, so I have relied on your intellect through much of this book.

During wartime combat a traditional axiom stated, it's always darkest before the dawn. It's always after a seemingly stretch of incomprehensible gibberish a bright light starts flashing and you are saying to yourself "well hell, that wasn't so hard."

The Kiss Method (Keep it simple stupid)
The easy way

In the first half of this book, you were exposed to my method of selecting stocks. If you are still a little fuzzy about selections as applied to selecting a portfolio, do yourself a favor and reread that portion again.

In the last chapter I will again emphasize the buying and selling of securities.

If you have followed my opinions and beliefs, you will find that your portfolio is top-heavy with momentum investments and not for the faint of heart. I have found that stocks that are the fastest risers are also the fastest losers.

Believe me you will have periods of gleeful euphoria and periods of unrelenting depression. So step into the world of derivative's where everything is magnified and now you are exposed to episodes that will manifest and accelerate past reactions to the current state of affairs.

My advice is, eliminate all easily reached implements of self-destruction before embarking on a career dedicated to option trading.

In the past, we may have been satisfied with returns of 20% and up weekly, monthly, or even yearly. In options, percentages many times surpass 50 % and more in a day or a week

I am an advocate of upward momentum but let's not forget value stocks that may have declined to levels that are unreasonable given their stock value at least in the eyes of pundit's that are ruminating about value as applied to that particular stock. Let's face it, they have no clue in hell whether that investment is going to rise or sink even further.

But we do know that the stock may have reached a price that is below what we think the value should be. Here is a position that may be ripe for an investment utilizing an option. We could buy a call, betting that the stock will go up in value in a certain period of time. We will lose our investment if it does not complete our expectations. We could sell a call betting it will not accelerate in value. In one case, we have created a "right" and in the other we have created an "obligation."

Illustration of **buying the call** option:
We use this if we are bullish on the stock.
Ulta Beauty,
Symbol Ulta

ULTA Jan 09 2019
9 Days to Expiration Jan 18 2019 the closing price.

Current stock price $280.79

Strike	Bid	Ask	Last
275.0 Call	9.70	10.30	10.16
277.5 Call	8.10	8.60	7.20
280.0 Call	6.70	7.10	6.78
282.5 Call	5.40	5.90	5.50
285.0 Call	4.30	4.80	4.80
287.5 Call	3.40	3.70	3.60

Simple to this point.

In this example, we will be buying a call, which gives me the right to buy Ulta at a specific price no matter how high the stock goes up.

Let's assume a strike price of 282.50. This would be an out of the money call expressed as OTM.

If Ulta ends 9 days from now at 300 we would exercise our right to buy it at 282.50.

Profit is $300
Minus $ 282.50

Gross profit $17.50
Premium $5.90

Net profit $11.60 on every share. Each Call is 100 shares. = $1,116 per contract not including commissions. At this time the commission at TD Ameritrade is $4.99 regardless of the number of contracts, but on each contract there is a cost per contract of 00.75 cents.

If the stock is not trading at expiration $282.50 or above we would probably not exercise our Right. Losing $5.90 per shares or $590.00 per contract not including commissions.

Now let's go the other way. Let's sell a call.

ULTA Jan 18 2019 7 Days to Expiration
Current price $281.50

Strike	Bid	Ask	Last
275.0 Call	8.60	9.30	7.90
277.5 Call	7.00	7.60	6.40
280.0 Call	5.60	6.10	5.98
282.5 Call	4.40	4.80	5.00
285.0 Call	3.30	3.70	3.30
287.5 Call	2.50	2.80	2.90

Again we are using Ulta Beauty and the expiration is only 7 days.

Select the same strike premium as in the prior example, 282.50.

Remember we are now selling a contract. Instead of a debit, it is now a credit.

Now I have created an obligation to sell Ulta at an OTM strike price of 282.50.

If the price of the stock does not exceed the strike, the entire premium is mine. +$4.80 per shares. Total $480

However if the stock goes to $300 as in the prior example, I will be obliged to sell the stock at the strike price.

My loss will be 300.00 -282.50

Gross loss

Per share - 17.50 predicated on 100 shares. Will be a total loss after deducting the premium of -12.50 per share. -$1,250 plus commissions.

In the above examples, I used the seven-day expiration options. These would be called weekly's. Not all stocks have weekly's. The most common would be thirty-day expiration options; however options can be in varying strikes and time periods extending to over a year.

Hold on to your hat, here we go to Put Options.

Selling Puts, this is one of my favorite investment plays.

Whenever a Put option is sold the money goes into your account. Of course that's true when selling a Call option too. The difference being the market tends to accelerate to higher levels as we have discussed before. This makes selling a Put almost a no-brainer if you are trading momentum stocks.

We will start with buying a Call; remember this is a debit to your account. It is a bull move.

Qualys Inc.
QLYS Feb 15 2019 32 Days to Expiration
Stock price per sh. 77.67

Strike	Bid	Ask	Last
65.0 Call	13.10	14.40	0.00
70.0 Call	9.10	10.10	0.00
75.0 Call	5.90	6.60	5.50
80.0 Call	3.30	3.90	3.11
85.0 Call	1.70	2.15	2.35
90.0 Call	.80	1.10	0.85

As an illustration let's select the 80 strike which means we would be $1.33 OTM. The ask is $3.90. But let's do a little bargaining and try to buy it at a price below the ask. Generally bidding a price half way between the bid and the ask is a good place to start. If we feel it's worth it we can always higher our price.

In this case buying as opposed to selling, we have acquired a "Right." The Right to sell Qlys anytime in the next 32days at a strike price of $80. Of course if the stock is selling below $80 it would not be to my advantage to exercise my Right. My loss will be $3.90 per sh... However in the event the investment has a good ride I would buy it at $80 and either hold the stock for possible future gains or promptly sell it locking in present gains whatever that would be. Realize Qlys would have to raise $3.90 plus $1.33 and be selling at $85.23 or higher to become a worthwhile purchase and don't forget commissions.

An investment that appeals to me is selling puts on momentum stocks. Below is an example of selling a put.

Utilizing the same stock as we did for Calls and the same time element, 32 days. The stock price is still $77.67.

Strike	Bid	Ask	Last
65.0 Put	1.00	1.25	1.00
70.0 Put	1.80	2.20	2.05
75.0 Put	3.30	3.90	3.30
80.0 Put	5.60	6.20	6.12
85.0 Put	7.70	9.80	0.00
90.0 Put	12.70	14.30	0.00

I have arbitrarily decided on the $75 dollar Put. The credit to our account will be $3.30.

If this stock stays above $75 we will have earned $330 per contract.

If the stock goes below $71.70 we will show a loss. You may be thinking going below $75 would start showing a loss but that is not true unless you ignore the $3.30 we received when selling the contract.

Advantages of selling Puts in this Market.
1) The amount you receive is a credit to your account and not a debit.
2) The market has generally been favoring advancement since 1939. Now don't get excited, I know there have been periods that were not favorable. By following the guidelines put forth in this book, with patience and some avarice you will experience much satisfaction in your investing life.
3) You have the ability to cover this position any time before the expiration date. Many times profits in excess of 100% can be obtained in one day.
4) I do not pretend to know with certainty what the future holds but I will always bet on America.
5) By using your intellectual abilities you can enhance profits or limit losses by using other calls and puts in combination with your original investment, or you can go long or short the underlying investment.
6) Flexibility can be extreme.

Example;

If I believed that Ultra would be going up in the near future than selling a Put and buying a call would be in my best interest.

However it is possible it may decline. How can I hedge my risk? Buy a put in conjunction with the selling of a put. That is a simple answer to a simple question. In this equation the money received from selling the Put is used to offset the premium on the Call. This strategy fits well with my philosophy of the acronym KISS!

I have another Philosophy called DAMN. This is the word I use to remind me "DAMN THE TORPEDOES, FULL STEAM AHEAD."

$ CHAPTER SEVEN $

Victory

Victory in the game of money requires a full set of orbs, or call it what you will, it simply means the inclination to take meaningful risks. In doing this you will inevitably lose on some investments but your gains will be much greater, after all that's the game plan.

Remember, for you this is the Super Bowl and you have no opponents. Everybody in this game is betting with you not against you. The one objective for everyone is to make money.

It is true that whenever you sell an option there is somebody on the other side of the transaction buying what you are selling, however it's a good bet that he has other options that he may be selling as well.

Remember, everybody wants you to win, including your stockbroker, the CEO, and other stockholders, your buddies, your mom and dad, your children and your wife and ex-wife and everyone you do business with. So, go get em cowboy were all pulling for you.

Keep in mind, selling a Call would be your best bet if after due consideration and utilizing the methods I have advocated previously, you find a stock that seems to be on a path to unenviable returns in the future. In other words, a stock that will probably be declining.

If you find a stock that the future is unlimited, than your best bet would be buying the stock and selling a put, or buying a call, personally my favorite move in the present market.

More than likely I would not buy a call. In this scenario having the call and the stock puts me in a position of duplicating an investment. In this case I want the stock as opposed to the call. The reason; there is a time limit on the call but not on the stock.

A word of caution, markets tend to rise and I personally would not be participating in markets that are having problems and the valuation is declining. If you find that the international situation is unclear or the Fed is issuing threatening statements or companies profit projections are not encouraging. Any number of things could be going on, putting a damper on expectations at the present time, it will behoove you to lighten the load in the manner that I have suggested and stay uncommitted until things become more favorable.

I say the foregoing with some trepidation. Personally I have been able to enhance my situation in declining markets.

With enough experience you may be able to emulate my ability to reach forward in down markets. Amazing things can be achieved if you have applied your God-given talents to them.

Make sure you use the Cornerstone "Prudence."

Investments that are declining will give off false indications of a turn in its potential, but you should remain patient and vigilant until you are positive a change has taken place.

One of the very favorable moves that you have available to you is the ability to start entering the market piece meal in drips and drabs. Large entities, insurance companies, mutual funds, banks, etc., are in a situation that forces them to enter an investment with massive amounts of capital. The problem they have is trying to be fully invested at all times. I realize it may be difficult to see this as a problem but believe me it is.

In your imagination, believe you are running in the North Atlantic alongside the Titanic. Your vessel is only 1/3 the size of the Titanic, both of you see the menacing Iceberg at the same time. The big ship tries to turn before ramming but there is not enough time, it's too big to turn quickly, you on the other-hand are able to quickly react because of your smaller size and avert a dire situation and avoid a calamity.

Did you know?
The sinking of the Titanic led to the creation of the U.S. Federal Reserve

www.facebook.com/Citizens.Action.Network

The novel *Futility*, an 1898 creation of Morgan Robertson, detailed the sinking of an unsinkable ship, the largest vessel afloat. This imaginary ship, named Titan, collided with an iceberg during April, resulting in a high loss of life because the ship carried too few lifeboats. Fourteen years later, with uncanny similarities, the real ship Titanic re-created what happened in the novel: The two ships had almost identical names; both ships were designated unsinkable; both were touted as the largest ships at sea; both collided with icebergs in April; both resulted in many deaths due to a shortage of lifeboats. Plus, both had strikingly similar floor plans and technical descriptions. Benjamin Guggenheim, Isador Strauss, the head of Macy's Department Stores, and John Jacob Astor, probably the wealthiest man in the world were all killed when it sank. Those three men were the main opposition to the creation of the U.S. Fed. By April, 1912, all opposition to the Federal Reserve was eliminated. In December of 1913, the Federal Reserve came into being in the United States controlled by the Illuminati Banksters.

Assume the amount, (in your infinite wisdom), you decide to invest is $50,000. Having done your due diligence and confident you have an unbelievable discovery that has no chance of declining in value. Think again, every investment, with enough time, ever promulgated on this planet has gone down at one time or another.

The proper way to approach this opportunity is to invest a small portion possibly 10% or an amount you are comfortable with and give this investment a chance to tell you what it wants to do. If after a period of time it shows instability, get rid of it and on to something else. Remember there are many attractive stocks in this universe. However if it gives off a smell of success than add to your venture in increments until you have reached an amount you are satisfied with.

I recall many years ago a well-researched stock I had been following for about six months. It was in the business of a-for profit educational institution, located in Chicago. After much trepidation I decided to finally invest. The time of day I entered the trade as I recall was twelve noon. The state of Illinois, exactly twenty minutes later raided the offices of this for Profit College and charged them with malfeasance and racketeering.

In twenty-five minutes I had lost 50% of my investment and fortunately was able to liquidate at that figure. At this point I could have given up and decided to relax in my future investing with CD"s or secure bonds or dividend stocks. My losses were not insignificant and at the time I needed every penny I could lay my hands on.

Unbelievably, my attitude became implausibly introspective and positive. I treated this incident as a lesson in my quest for a successful eventual result. It would have been so easy to listen to my wife and friends and followed a different path, one not so encumbered with obstacles, and one that I could never achieve the type of success I desired.

Remember the cornerstones. Follow your dreams utilizing Prudence and never ever lose your ambition and drive. Believe in yourself.

Blind ambition is not what I'm talking about, but intelligent and well thought out response to obstructions in the winner's road.

Speaking of high risk, Options are a very fascinating and alluring addition to your portfolio. They should not be the main attraction. On first blush, the percentage gains that can be attained with these instruments can be highly intoxicating. If carried to extremes, will be detrimental to your goals.

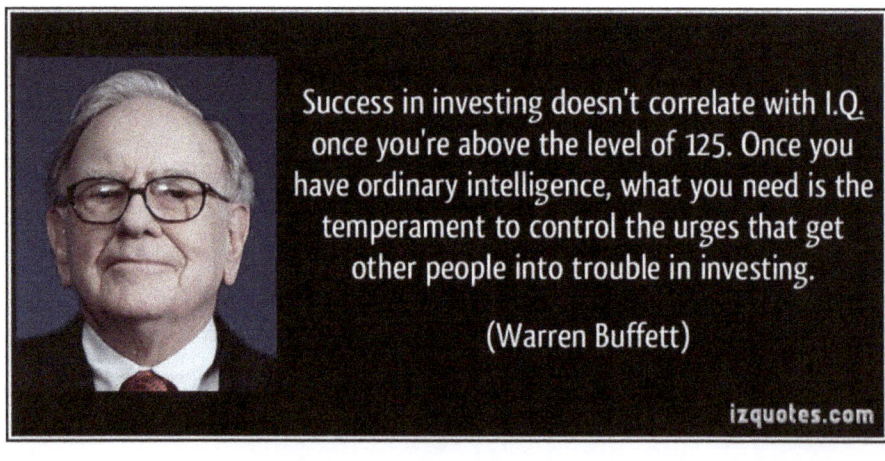

Options are derivatives of actual securities but remember they are ephemeral in nature. They exist in their own cocoon and burst into a beautiful Butterfly or die and whither on the vine. Both scenarios will occur in your wheelhouse.

Recently I was viewing a financial show on television. A panel of experts were having a discussion about the current state of the market. This conversation took place in the latter part of December 2018 and the market was deeply in the doldrums. As the spotlight came to one particular panelist the interviewer remarked that the panelist was not his usual ebullient self, spouting off about the stocks he's recommending. He, the panelist looked at the interviewer very much with a hangdog look and said, "It's true, I presently have no answers; I've been trampled by the market." At that moment this seer went up many points in my estimation of this gentleman, because of his honesty.

Yes it's true, when the market starts its downward slide even the most knowledgeable stock market mavens will most likely suffer along with their devotees. Unless they are the rare individual that can turn on a dime and change their complete Philosophy and become overnight bears. That means going into unfamiliar territory and don't give a damn about the historical ramifications of the securities industry.

Intrinsic Value and Time value as applied to Options.

Intrinsic value simply means the actual value of the stock if it is in the money. Assume a stock is trading at $52 and a put option at a strike of $50 is trading at $4, we would consider that $2 is the intrinsic value and $2 is the time value.

As the option draws nearer its strike price the time value will decrease in value and the intrinsic value will always be whatever the value of the stock is as long it is still in the money. However it can never be a minus value.

This brings up another reason I prefer selling as opposed to buying an option. When selling an option you receive the time value as well as the intrinsic value. When buying an option you are paying for the time value and intrinsic value assuming the option is in the money.

Actions on acquired options you need to be aware of and need to take prior to expiration of option positions:

Log in to your account to review your expiring positions. Determine if you need to take action to:

Avoid an exercise or assignment of your options, or

Ensure you have adequate money in your account to carry any stock positions if there is an exercise or assignment of your options.

Review any adjustments you may have already made to make sure there is nothing else you need to do at this time.

Please keep in mind, holding positions in your account which could potentially cause significant risk, such as a low-equity situation, margin call, cash debit, IRA debit, or short positions. It is your responsibility to trade out of any position your account cannot support due to an exercise or assignment.

Investing in Stocks is the world's best Tax Shelter

In my world, paying gobs of taxes was a sign of victory in the game of money. I will have to concede to having a bit of childish mindless amusement.

When you reach a stage in life that everything you might want, you already have, you will find other small diversions to occupy your time.

When indulging in small diversions keep in mind whatever you do, having substantial assets makes you a target of unwanted lawsuits and harassments that can take large bites of your time and resources.

Owning stock puts you in a unique position of never having to pay taxes for untold years on your profits. Taxes on stocks in the market are not counted until they become in a liquid position.

Rule of 72

$1,000 dollars invested utilizing the rule of 72 and choosing an arbitrary 10% rate of return would produce a 7.2 number of years it would take our $1,000 to double too $2,000 in value. To produce the number of years, simply divide the interest rate into 72 and voila you have the answer. If you are required to pay the government what he figures is his fair share, on that $1,000 you will be left with approximately $800. Utilizing the rule of 72 at an interest rate of 10% will take you 7.2 years to double to $1600.

I think you can see that tax avoidance is an important concept but not at the expense of keeping an investment in a vegetative state long past the time it should have been liquidated.

Assume $1,000 invested now and each year $1,000 a total of 21 years @ 10% at the end of 21 years comes to 64,002.50, without paying federal taxes. Of course we must assume that Uncle Sam would not look favorably if we avoided paying our fair share in his estimation. If we assume that we pay 15% a year on that $1,000 our total invested each year would be $150 less. Total amount after taxes $56,671.87 a difference of $17,330.63.

It is possible to avoid taxes for 21 years, simply buy a stock investment, and keep it for 21 years.

Some of you may be wondering where you can receive 10% a year? The simple answer; any half way decent growth mutual fund will return at least that amount over a period of years.

That brings us to the subject of this book. I do not give a damn about taxes. My only object is to make money as quickly as possible, with a reasonable safety factor. If that means using short-term securities, and paying taxes, then so be it. As a matter of fact I consider it a success if the taxes I pay each year would be considered sizable.

Penny stocks are not in my bailiwick, if you are looking for stocks that are selling for small amounts of capital, you are reading the wrong book. Everything that I do in most cases, are directed to substantial companies with significant capital to build on and fund future growth.

I have felt, in the majority of cases, anything we buy of quality has a higher price tag than one of lower quality. Stocks generally fall in the same category. Look at a $1 stock and a $100 stock do you see a difference. The markets mechanism in most cases will price a security in tandem with the prevailing value of that company. The exception to this rule is the value of momentum stocks. This throws a spotlight on my method of investing.

It is worth repeating, the higher the rate of return the higher the velocity and greater degree of loss. The word velocity I included in that statement to enable me to emphasize the probability that a diminishing market will be a faster movement downward than its ability to increase with equal speed. So it becomes imperative your ability to herald the coming decline is unimpeded. In this book, I have highlighted the way to handle increases and decreases in value. If you must, reread those chapters.

Hark back to the part of this book that emphasizes the roll your personal philosophy plays in this scenario.

I have recently had an unfortunate experience concerning a stock I held in a degree of loftiness. Its primary Industry concerned clothing apparel. Movement of this security was rapidly increasing and of course my inclination was to purchase a greater amount along the way. As their reporting of profit and loss came to past, it was as I expected, all of the numbers I placed the greatest faith in, turned out to be boffo except for one little expectation, the earnings for the coming quarters and next year were a little on the dreary side and because it did not meet the expected projections, the price of the stock declined about 15%. This dented my pocket book. I felt at the time and still do, that the decline was excessive. Being that I was in possession of the stock and a naked put option on the selling side with the strike date fast approaching, I decided to cover the option and keep the stock. Upon deeper reflection, I decided to eliminate both. My thinking; fool me once shame on you, fool me twice shame on me.

The ending of that story; I was correct the stock continued sagging. I do feel that this stock will eventually turn around, but in the meantime, I'm getting older. There are other fish in the sea, let's put a new wiggly worm on the line and cast about in the other part of the sea and try to find that one giant fish. I'm sure he's out there.

$ CHAPTER EIGHT $

Life is Lived only Once

I have heard it said,
 The book of life is brief and once a page is turned, it will never be read in the same way again. That page is

dead and as each page is turned, it brings you closer to the finality of life.

So it is true, life is lived only once. How much time do you have to accomplish all that you need to do?

Reading this book I hope, has been an adventure you will carry with you for the rest of your life. I understand many times this compendium has been incomprehensible, but I have tried to distill what has made me successful in my 85 years of life in so few pages.

Well, that is the last conundrum. It's neither probable nor possible to condense all I want to relate to you in this tiny compilation of truths, facts, and methods, I have found to be the cornerstone's I have lived by. So Be it, it will have to do.

The one cornerstone I found to be the most helpful while writing this book;

The book of knowledge.

Let History be your Instructor

You may think of history as archaic, decrepit, hoary, riddled with green mossy stuff and known instances of boredom found in the institutes of this nation.

You would be wrong. Just open the Book of Knowledge. It is filled with history, the only place that all wisdom has been assembled.

What's that you say? It doesn't apply to me. Wow, wrong again!

If you want to be successful in any endeavor; make a study of history. If you become proficient and immersed in the art of antiquity you will find the relevance of this book to be lessened. My attempt here is to capture the essence of investing. Every bit of wisdom disseminated here, has been cultivated from the pages of the Book of Knowledge.

"Hello! What's that you say? You're kidding, the book of knowledge? Never heard of it. Where can I find this book and who the hell wrote it?"

If you want to find that manuscript, it is easily accessible in thousands of buildings across this country. Written by thousands and thousands of scholars, intellectuals, and knowledgeable noted issue of scions, it's called a "Library" Look in the history section.

$ CHAPTER NINE $

(No… This is not a mistake. Because of its importance I have decided to recap chapter four.)

Finding Growth Stocks

If you have established an account through a reputable brokerage firm, they generally provide you with lists of stocks that they have vetted and placed in categories, i.e. high yield, conservative, large cap, small cap, growth, etc.

There are other places that willingly provide stocks in diverse classifications and are freely provided. In fact there are so many that you will be virtually inundated with choices.

Area's that interest us, are growth, large cap, small cap, and speculative.

As you peruse these lists find names that you may have a kissing relationship. Possibly general merchandise stores, factories where you have bought something from, drug chains, manufacturing plants, furniture, tv.'s, computer's, you get the idea. Having well-established companies such as Proctor and Gamble or McDonald's can be very comforting in your portfolio. Companies that pay a healthy dividend are also very comforting, however owning this type of investment will probably not bring in millions of dollars in compensation. A comprehensive list of high tech innovative companies can also be compiled this way. Settle on four or five, if you have the time look over a few more.

Look at their chart patterns, the one's that show a generally increasing pattern upward will be selected for further investigation. Be aware the construction of a chart can be misleading. A chart that has a steep upward progression may not be as significant as one that has a flatter trajectory. As time goes on you will have a practiced eye that gives immediate results.

So now you have settled on a few of these candidates for enshrinement in the hall of fame, find out exactly what they do. Companies can surprise you. What you thought they did may not be their major source of income. It is to your benefit to have an understanding of their role in business.

Your individual self comes to us packed with many biases, some are good some are bad and some occupy a semblance of neutrality. This book has not the time or the expertise to enhance or disparage your prejudices. I must make sure that they do not influence and get in the way of what we are trying to achieve, namely enhancing our pocketbook.

Knowing where a company gets most of its marble's gives us an inkling that we can juxtapose on to our understanding of life as we know it. This is where our judgement takes over and tells us if the product they are purveying is of importance as we see it.

Once you have decided on the company or companies you have selected, our next objective is to find out if anybody gives a damn about them. You can find this information on the bottom of most charts. It's the number of shares traded in a certain period of time, for instance one month, three months, six months. If the stock is trending upward with a corresponding increase in the volume of shares being traded, is a good indication this stock will probably continue on an upward path. If the reverse is true it may be on its way downward.

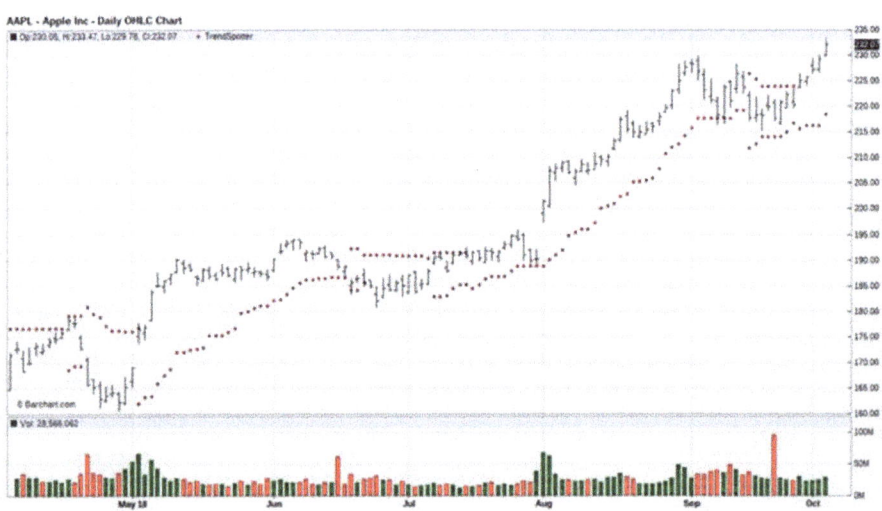

The above chart shows a stock moving in the proper direction.

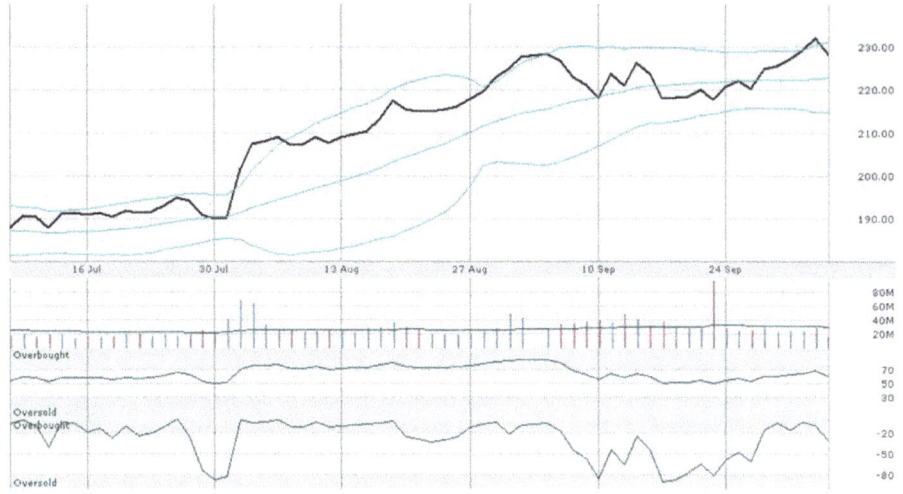

Chart showing Bollinger bands

In all scenarios the prevailing wind may suddenly turn directions and that will happen inevitably in a certain percentage of the cases. Your impulse is directed by the amount of experience you have in charting and deciphering what the company does, its top line, bottom line, up or down volume and the direction and volatility in the trading and pricing of its shares. Another indicator we can use is called Bollinger bands. Make your own independent study of this indicator. It may help in your decision-making.

    As an example; a stock we own trades at $22 dollars. Its variance for a few days is $22.50, $22.25, $ 21.90, $20.78 $19.99, now our experience and intuition takes over. Remember a few days does not a pattern of trading make. It's not just the pricing that matters it's the

229 |Visionary Trader

complete picture. All of the foregoing now comes into play. Eventually you will be able to make literally instantaneous decisions. It does not matter if you are right or wrong; action may be required.

The amount of inertia that takes place finally decides how much money comes to you. If you follow conventional wisdom; take your time; analyze each aspect of the trade ad nauseaum into infinity. If you are standing at the water's edge and don't move around you will slowly sink into the sand.

An incidence that transpired in my home brought this cornerstone to mind vividly. A friend and his wife that stayed for the weekend whom we have many things in common and of course investing in stocks and options was a prime conversation piece.

Naturally in the course of writing this book our conversation turned to investing utilizing my methods. I knew him to be a consummate investor. During that weekend he wanted to experience my techniques. I gladly accommodated his request to use my method to help him in his quest to improve his selection of investments.

Sunday was spent brainstorming what we decided would be the securities to be taken advantage of Monday morning. In this case we were looking at selling naked put options which are a derivative of particular stocks which I have covered in detail in this book. My friend departed early Monday morning traveling to their home in South Carolina.

As soon as trading began at 9:30 a.m. I immediately made the trades we had decided on the day before. Within a two-hour period I had earned over nine hundred dollars and kept these investments for expiration in five days and earned in excess of one thousand five hundred dollars. I called him later that week expecting to be congratulated and a thank you, but neither was forthcoming because he never executed the trades.

Believing he could get a better price, consequently he delayed taking advantage of an opportunity that was right in front of him. It was not just him but most people will trip over dollars to pick up nickels. It was not just the opportunity that was lost but his inability to see the bigger picture as more than likely many chances had been lost through his intransigence.

Examples of this type are legend, they are almost too numerous to mention.

The simple way.
To make as much money as you want.

KISS
Keep It Simple Stupid
1) Pick four or five new stock investments.
2) Check their chart (Should be rising for the last month.)

3) Top line must be ascending 10 plus percent per quarter.
4) Volume increasing.
5) Recent news on the investment is benign.
6) Select the pick of the litter.
7) Buy 15 to 25% of the amount you are intending to invest.
8) If the security is ascending in a steady pattern, continue to acquire more shares up to your limit.
9) As an adjunct to the security, sell Put Options on the base investment.
10) Remember, use your intelligence. THINK!

Many of readers will have a disagreement with me on buying or trading a stock that has been on a tear, preferring to purchase that entity after somewhat of a pull back on the share price.

Actually, I am in accordance with that philosophy if the stock has been showing strength prior to a decline in value. This many times is what happens in the normal course of events.

After a large run-up in price, many traders will be taking profits.

$ CHAPTER TEN $

Ramifications of Old Age

I don't know if I am correct but I worry about dying. Actually not just dying from any old thing, but specifically dying from old age. I am at the age that most of the people I knew in my life have passed away. I worry not just about dying of old age but if I do survive to a much older age what will be the consequence's, Walker's, crutches, wheelchairs, can't see, can't hear, don't recognize people or friends, can't dance anymore, no dreams and nothing to look forward too except more physical pain, more hospital stays.

Possibly, God forbid, Joanie my companion of twenty-seven years may precede me. I'll end up in a home with somebody feeding me. I could go on and on. Yes, that is what worries me.

I do believe that the only cure is to try as hard as I can to not think about it and take life one day at a time. But that's not me. I still have hopes and dreams. I want to be much wealthier than I am. I want to be able to travel on my own personal plane, I want to leave behind a legacy of some type, I want to finish the book I am working on, I want Joanie to have a great life, I want my son and his wife to have all the things that are important to them There are so many things to do yet but it just seems that little by little I am in the process of dying. I know that no one gets out of this life alive.

Yes, the grim reaper is standing in the road waiting. The most important thing for me is to stay busy and be a man and face what I have to face, as all of us must. That is an inescapable truth.

When we reach an Advanced Age

If we have followed the prudent path in life and have accumulated the wherewithal to afford most of the extravagant things that will make our life if not enjoyable at least affordable, old age will become tolerable.

Things like:
- Assisted care for you and your wife in a facility of your choice, not a government provided indigent care resource.
- Total full time care in your own home.
- Advances in medicine that becomes available.
- Leave a legacy to your children and take the burden for your care off their shoulders.
- Grand children can be educated in the finest colleges, funded by you.

If you have taken the necessary steps, your declining years will be bearable. Possibly at times enjoyable.

Remember **Money** is the catalyst.

The author and significant other
at their Island home in Florida
Ron Chicone and Joan Lyons

Addendum

Pursuing and fulfilling our destiny, many times requires a degree of flexibility and may not have been exhibited in prior exhortations in this manuscript.

There are times events occur that were never anticipated in the normal course of expected outcomes. When these happenings result in unexpected losses, we must reestablish our reasoned judgements that led to the decisions we formulated in the past concerning that venture.

Let's assume a highly speculative investment went down 17% in a short period of time and exceeded my limit of minus 10% loss from its last high. You may decide after examining the trading history of this investment, in other words, its past history, indicates that a purchase of additional shares is specified or you may possibly be thinking of other actions to pursue. You will not be wrong as long as your action is a considered prudent judgement.

Realize in the above scenario, the better part of valor would be to take the current situation and sell some of it or all of it and move on.

Many of you who are eagerly reading this book are doing so hoping to spend as little time as possible on actually trading stocks and doing gobs of research, especially those of you that are employed in the health care field or officers in a company that demands much of your time. Those are not the only fields that the time element is precious, some people feel that spending time with their families supersedes all else and there's certainly nothing wrong with that. Something I heartily endorse.

The question becomes, can you experience the same degree of success spending less time researching the various avenues to victory in the pursuit of money? Yes you can. There are those that consider hands off a superior method of investing.

In my own experience, because of time constraints, I have had to ignore a particular portfolio and when I did, I performed better sitting on the sidelines rather than being an active participant. However, in most cases I was in a better position when I was aware of the ramifications of a particular security. E.g. Top line, bottom line, shares traded and political implications which can affect the entire market.

So, what are the ironclad rules that are written in stone that will bring the market to an empirical closure?

If you have paid attention as you were reading this book, then you already know the answer.

THEY DO NOT EXIST.

To those of you who are desperately searching for crutches to help through this jungle land of conundrums and contradictions, I refer you to the "Cornerstones," particularly, Prudence, Imagination, Morality, and let history be your instructor.

In closing, I have given you the keys to a life filled with excitement, exhilaration, and riches.

Now, open that secret door, step through it and you are standing on the threshold of dreams fulfilled.

Ron Chicone

Please check out other fine books by Ron Chicone

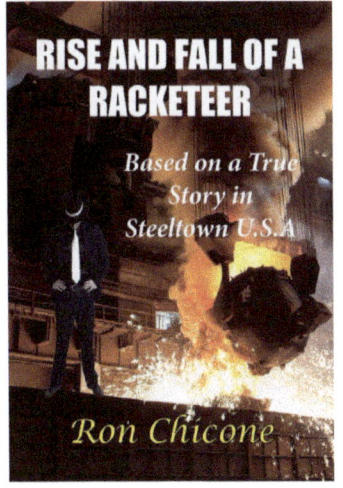

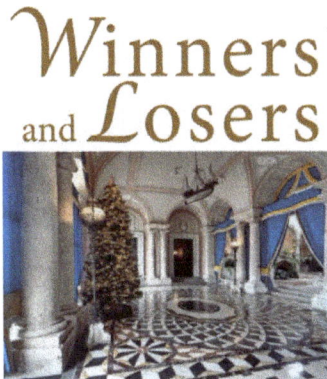

www.ingramcontent.com/pod-product-compliance
Lightning Source LLC
Chambersburg PA
CBHW040309170426
43195CB00020B/2903